MERIDIAN

Crossing Aesthetics

Werner Hamacher

Editor

D1382911

Stanford
University
Press

———

Stanford
California
2005

INHERITING THE FUTURE

INHERITING THE FUTURE

Legacies of Kant,
Freud, and Flaubert

Elizabeth Rottenberg

Stanford University Press
Stanford, California

Printed in the United States of America on acid-free, archival-quality paper

Library of Congress Cataloging-in-Publication Data

Rottenberg, Elizabeth, 1969–
    Inheriting the future : legacies of Kant, Freud, and Flaubert / Elizabeth Rottenberg.
        p. cm.
    Includes bibliographical references and index.
    ISBN 0-8047-5113-7 (cloth : alk. paper) – ISBN 0-8047-5114-5 (pbk. : alk. paper)
    1. Moral conditions in literature.   2. Ethics in literature.   3. European literature–18th century–History and criticism.   4. European literature–19th century–History and criticism.   5. Kant, Immanuel, 1724–1804–Criticism and interpretation.   6. Freud, Sigmund, 1856–1939–Criticism and interpretation.   7. Flaubert, Gustave, 1821–1880–Criticism and interpretation.   I. Title.
    PN56.M59R68   2005
    809'.93353–dc22
                                                                                            2004030247

Typeset by TechBooks in 10.9/13 Adobe Garamond

Original Printing 2005

Last figure below indicates year of this printing:
14 13 12 11 10 09 08 07 06 05

To Ari

Acknowledgments

Above all, I wish to thank Cathy Caruth whose brilliant insight has been the source of so much inspiration and guidance. My thanks also to Danielle Follett whose unrelenting good sense has taught me the consolation of philosophy.

Contents

Note on Sources and Key to Abbreviations and Translations

Kant

Apart from the *Critique of Pure Reason*, all references to Kant are to *Kants Gesammelte Schriften* (Ak), ed. Königliche Preussische (later Deutsche) Akademie der Wissenschaften, 29 volumes (Berlin and Leipzig: Walter de Gruyer, 1902). References to the *Critique of Pure Reason* are to the standard A and B pagination of the first and second editions. Specific works cited in the main body of the text are referred to by means of the abbreviations listed below; those cited only in the notes are given with full title. The translations used are listed as follows and, except in the case of the *Critique of Pure Reason*, are referred to immediately following the reference to the German text. It should be noted that I have silently modified the English translations throughout. Where there is no reference to an English translation, the translation is my own.

A/B   *Kritik der reinen Vernunft* (Ak 3 and 4).
   Critique of Pure Reason, trans. Norman Kemp Smith (New York: St. Martin's Press, 1965).

Gr   *Grundlegung zur Metaphysik der Sitten* (Ak 4: 387–463).
   Grounding for the Metaphysics of Morals, trans. James M. Ellington (Indianapolis: Hackett, 1993).

KprV *Kritik der praktischen Vernunft* (Ak 5: 1–163).
      Critique of Practical Reason, trans. L. W. Beck (Indianapolis: Bobbs-Merrill, 1956).

MS   *Die Metaphysik der Sitten* (Ak 6: 203–493).
      The Metaphysics of Morals, trans. Mary Gregor (Cambridge: Cambridge University Press, 1991).

Rel   *Die Religion innerhalb der Grenzen der bloßen Vernunft* (Ak 6: 1–202).
      Religion within the Limits of Reason Alone, trans. Theodore M. Greene and Hoyt H. Hudson (New York: Harper and Row, 1960).

SF   *Der Streit der Fakultäten* (Ak 7: 1–116).
      The Conflict of the Faculties, trans. Mary Gregor (Lincoln: University of Nebraska Press, 1979).

Auf   "Beantwortung der Frage: Was ist Aufklärung?" (Ak 8: 33–42).
      "An Answer to the Question: 'What Is Enlightenment?'" *Political Writings*, ed. Hans Reiss, trans. H. B. Nisbet (Cambridge: Cambridge University Press, 1970), 54–60.

Ton   *Von einem neuerdings erhobenen vornehmen Ton in der Philosophie* (Ak 8: 387–406).
      "On a Newly Arisen Superior Tone in Philosophy," *Raising the Tone of Philosophy*, ed. and trans. Peter Fenves (Baltimore: Johns Hopkins University Press, 1993), 51–72.

DO   "Was heißt: sich im Denken orientieren?" (Ak 8: 131–47).
      "What Is Orientation in Thinking?" *Political Writings*, ed. Hans Reiss, trans. H. B. Nisbet (Cambridge: Cambridge University Press, 1970), 237–49.

Freud

All translations of Freud's work will refer to *The Standard Edition of the Complete Psychological Works of Sigmund Freud*, translated from the German under the general editorship of James Strachey in collaboration with Anna Freud, assisted by Alix Strachey and Alan Tyson, 24 volumes (London: The Hogarth Press, 1953–1974). For a critical discussion of the Standard Edition's translations, see Bruno Bettelheim's 1982 article in *The New Yorker*, "Freud and the Soul," 1 March 1982, 52–93. All references to this edition will be abbreviated SE followed by volume and page number. German references will be to Freud's *Gesammelte Werke*, 18 volumes (Frankfurt am Main: Fischer Verlag, 1999). I have silently modified the Standard Edition translations throughout.

Flaubert

For all letters written after 1875 (and therefore not available in Jean Bruneau's Pléiade edition), I have referred to the Conard second edition of Flaubert's letters and its supplement. For correspondence with Guy de Maupassant, George Sand, and Ivan Turgeniev, I have used the excellent collections published by Flammarion. All translations of Flaubert's correspondence are my own. In the case of *Bouvard et Pécuchet* where two page numbers are given, the first always refers to the French edition of the text. I have silently modified the Earp and Stonier translation throughout.

BP   *Bouvard et Pécuchet*, ed. Claudine Gothot-Mersch (Paris: Gallimard, 1979). *Bouvard and Pécuchet*, trans. T. W. Earp and G. W. Stonier (New York: New Directions, 1954).

CB   *Correspondance*, ed. Jean Bruneau, 4 vols. (Paris: Gallimard, 1973–1998).

CC   *Correspondance*, 9 vols. (Paris: Conard, 1926–1933).

GM   *Correspondance Gustave Flaubert–Guy de Maupassant*, ed. Yvan Leclerc (Paris: Flammarion, 1993).

GS   *Correspondance Gustave Flaubert–George Sand*, ed. Alphonse Jacobs (Paris: Flammarion, 1981).

IT   *Correspondance Gustave Flaubert–Ivan Tourguéniev,* ed. Alexandre Zviguilsky (Paris: Flammarion, 1989).

S   *Correspondance,* Supplement, eds. René Dumesnil, Jean Pommier, and Claude Digeon, 4 vols. (Paris: Conard, 1954).

Je größer das Denkwerk eines Denkers ist, das sich keineswegs mit dem Umfang und der Anzahl seiner Schriften deckt, um so reicher ist das in diesem Denkwerk Ungedachte, d.h. jenes, was erst und allein durch dieses Denkwerk als Noch-nicht-Gedachtes heraufkommt.

—(Martin Heidegger, *Der Satz vom Grund*)

The greater the work of a thinker—which in no way corresponds to the scope and number of his writings—the richer is that which is unthought in this work, namely, that which for the first time and through this work rises to the surface as having not-yet-been-thought.

—(Martin Heidegger, *The Principle of Reason*)

Prefatory Note

In French law, there is a saying: "le mort saisit le vif" (the dead invests the living). In this adage, the verb "saisir" (to seize) not only expresses the power of the dead over the living. It also refers to a right, the legal right of a living person— "la saisine" (*Code civil,* article 724)—that goes into effect immediately upon the death of a testator. Indeed, as we will see, this legal use of the verb "saisir" translates one of the most fundamental principles of hereditary acquisition. Inheritance confers on me a right, and this right is exclusive because the authorization to accept belongs to me alone. The right to an inheritance is not a possession, however, and it should not be confused with an unqualified gain or even with something whose desirability can be assumed. Rather the exclusive authorization to choose whether I will or will not have the legacy in question is "mine" regardless of my choice; my desire to be possessed of such a choice has no bearing on the possibility of my chosenness. The right to accept or refuse a legacy is not something I choose. It is my election to the necessity of choice.

When it occurs, an act of inheritance (the acceptance of a legacy) is an extraordinary act: on the one hand, because it elicits from the heir a response to a chosenness; on the other hand, because any true act of inheritance always implies momentous decisions and responsibilities. Until there is a decision on the part of the heir, a legacy cannot but remain suspended, hovering between acceptance and rejection.

Inheriting the Future explores the implicit but unarticulated relation between legacy and morality. If every act of inheritance requires decision and responsibility, then the question "What should I do?" is no longer simply discursive or theoretical: it is also moral. But let us not forget that the critical concept of moral possibility comes to us from Kant who literally refers to it as a bequest, a "Vermächtnis" of speculative reason. This book examines the notion of morality in the late work of Kant and analyzes its nineteenth and twentieth century extensions in the writings of Flaubert and Freud. In all three writers, I suggest, the definition of morality is bound up with this more fundamental problem of legacy. Kant's analysis of "possession," Freud's study of obsessional neurosis, and Flaubert's stylistic innovations thus require us to rethink the concept of autonomy in terms of an inheritance that is not "ours" to refuse.

Beginning with Kant's distinction between an external object of choice and an object of respect that "possesses" a dignity, Chapter 1 points to an example of "possession" that not only lies beyond the concept of ownership but also conditions the very possibility of moral action. Chapter 2 then turns to the case of obsessional neurosis in Freud—to that illness where those affected seem possessed by a peculiar force of super-moral obligation. Finally, in the posthumous work of Flaubert, Chapter 3 investigates the legacy of a narrative temporality that forces us onward, indefinitely, relentlessly, in the name of "sameness."

Because the structure of inheritance gestures beyond philosophy, psychoanalysis, and literature, this book does not simply focus on three authors, it also covers three centuries and three disciplines. One might further speculate that legacies—because they exceed all traditional notion of boundary—*always* speak in more than one voice (idiom, language). Indeed, as I have tried to show, every legacy points to a structural predicament, a fissure that forever prevents what we call "epistemology" from closing itself off in spatiotemporal terms. The question of legacy is not simply a question that is left to the future: it is *the* question that *must be* left to the future. And yet, as attested by the examples of Kant, Freud, and Flaubert in this book, a legacy is also an ongoing obligation to which we are bound to respond.

Introduction

Of Human Bondage

Back to the Future

What is the moral legacy of the Enlightenment? How, to use Kant's 1784 definition of "Aufklärung," has *"man's emergence* [Ausgang] *from his self-incurred immaturity* [aus seiner selbstverschuldeten Unmündigkeit]" (Auf 33; 54) left its mark on the twentieth century? Are we to remember the Enlightenment as but a moment of "shallow and pretentious intellectualism" characterized by "individualistic tendencies" and an "unreasonable contempt for tradition and authority" as we read in the most recent edition of the Oxford English Dictionary? Or is there perhaps at the heart of the Enlightenment another Enlightenment: one that not only gestures beyond the "individualistic tendencies" of the Enlightenment and its "contempt for tradition" but also—precisely because it always gestures beyond the Enlightenment—comes to us through its heirs?

Freud, I will suggest, is one of the Enlightenment's truest heirs in this sense. Indeed, in his controversial and unsettling book *The Future of an Illusion* (1928), Freud issues a indictment of religion so scathing that it is rivaled only by the devastating attack on religion's claims to supersensible knowledge that we find in Kant's critical philosophy. All religious ideas, Freud contends in this book, are illusions—dangerous to reality and motivated solely by wish-fulfillment. And yet in this most anti-religious of treatises, Freud ends up pointing to something in reason itself that takes us beyond the scientific grounds from which he launches his attack. In this text that condemns our psychical need to humanize the nonhuman forces of the external world, in a manifesto that equates religious belief with a kind of neurotic infantilism, there is, I will argue, a trace of something distinctly moral. Moreover, as we will see, Freud's concept of reason not only points to a strange "common compulsion," it also links this compulsion to a notion of right and futurity.

No civilization can decide *never* to make further progress in its thinking just as no religion can decide never to reform its churches. It simply does not have the "right," says Freud. No people can make such a decision because a decision of this kind—in the words of Kant this time—"would be opposed to the humanity in their own persons and so to the highest Right of the people"(MS 327–28; 137). Freud's "common compulsion" in *The Future of an Illusion*, I will argue, brings to mind the Enlightenment in its insistent call to reason, but also, I would claim, in its recognition of something whose grounds are no longer to be found in objective knowledge. Freud's recourse to a "common compulsion," I will suggest, repeats Kant's positing of a "cognitive drive" in "What Is Orientation in Thinking?" (1786). At the heart of *The Future of an Illusion*, in other words, lies a thoroughly Kantian legacy.

At the root of a psychological "compulsion [*Zwang*]" lies the history of a philosophical "drive [*Trieb*]." Indeed, with this shift from psychology to philosophy, we pass from a critique of the human need for psychical mastery (for a closed cognitive system) to another and more enigmatic need: the need of reason *not* to be reinscribed within a cognitive system. Only by returning to the Enlightenment, I will suggest, do we emerge from it with new, more enigmatic, moral insight.

A Tale of Two Cities

I begin with two examples, the juxtaposition of which will help lay the groundwork for the relation between Freud and Kant. What lies in the future, says Freud, is the primacy of the intellect. Although the voice of the intellect is soft, "it does not rest until it has gained a hearing [*sie ruht nicht, ehe sie sich Gehör geschafft hat*]."[1] Indeed, this restlessness, according to Freud, is "one of the few points on which one may be optimistic about the future [*in denen man für die Zukunft der Menschheit optimistisch sein darf*]" (SE 21: 87). The primacy of the intellect (*der Primat des Intellekts*) is our best hope for the future, even if this future is only a distant one.

What thwarts the progress of civilization and represents its greatest danger is religion. In spite of their incontrovertible lack of authentication, Freud marvels, religious doctrines have always exerted the strongest possible influence on humankind. What is so remarkable, says Freud, is the sheer inner force of doctrines whose effectiveness is wholly independent "of recognition by reason [*von der vernünftigen Anerkennung*]" (SE 21: 45). Religion—or that "most important item in the psychical inventory of a civilization" (SE 21: 18)—is so effective, Freud explains, because it ministers to the narcissistic needs of human beings. Religious teachings are not "precipitates of experience or end-results of thinking [*Niederschläge der Erfahrung oder Endresultate des Denkens*]": they are illusions through and through, but they are also, at the same time, "fulfillments of the oldest, strongest and most urgent wishes of mankind" (SE 21: 47).

The relationship between civilization and religion must undergo a fundamental revision for there to be a future. Although religious teachings may at times resemble other kinds of teaching that lay claim to our belief and tell us something about the world, they must be distinguished from them. When we are told, for example, that "the town on Konstanz lies on the Bodensee" (SE 21: 37–38), anyone who does not believe it can always "go and see" and thereby verify the correctness of the assertion. Unlike religious teachings, assertions of a historical nature "demand belief in their contents," but not without producing *grounds* for their claims (SE 21: 38–39).

In "What Is Orientation in Thinking?" (1786), Kant presents us with an example of belief identical in form to Freud's Konstanz example. Again this example is used to illustrate the difference

between a belief whose grounds for considering something to be
true "are by nature devoid of all objective validity" and a belief whose
grounds are objective but are "consciously regarded as inadequate"
(DO 141; 244). Only in the latter case can the belief in question
ever be transformed into knowledge:

> It is therefore perfectly consistent that something should be consid-
> ered historically true purely on the strength of testimonies [*bloß auf
> Zeugnisse*], as in the belief that there is a city called Rome and the fact
> that someone who has never been there should nevertheless be able to
> say '*I know*' and not just '*I believe* that Rome exists.' (DO 141; 244)

Like the Konstanz example in Freud, the Rome example[2] here
moves easily between belief and knowledge. In both cases, historical belief is based on objective grounds of knowledge. In neither
case, therefore, is historical belief the kind of belief that is under
discussion.

And yet, the Rome example in Kant's argument serves a completely different function from that of the Konstanz example in
Freud's. For Kant, the example of a belief that can become knowledge is not a strong example of the production of objective grounds
but, on the contrary, a weak example (even a counterexample) of the
production of subjective ones. The belief that there is a city called
Rome is not a strong example of belief because the belief can eventually become knowledge. In this way, the belief that Rome exists
serves only as a foil for the belief that is to be treated as the *opposite*
of knowledge: namely, the belief that can never become knowledge
and which Kant calls a "rational belief" (*Vernunftglaube*). Instead
of leading us to the primacy of intellect, in effect, Kant's example already indicates a possibility beyond objective principles of
reason.

For Kant the notion of "rational belief" is not opposed to reason. Rather it emerges from reason, from a need "inherent in reason
itself" (DO 136; 240). Although a "rational belief" must be distinguished from "an insight capable of fulfilling all the logical requirements for certainty"—indeed, a "need" must never be regarded

as an "insight"—the conviction of truth of a rational belief is "not inferior in degree to knowledge . . . even if it is totally different from it in kind" (DO 141; 245). I will suggest in what follows that "rational belief" is not only a necessary presupposition for finite rational beings, as Kant argues, but also a rational remainder of a need that could begin to account for the inaugural grounding or founding of speculative reason itself. Since this rational remainder is not accessible to speculative reason, as we will see, it is only ever conveyed through it. Indeed, as it turns out, it is to this rational remainder that Freud's "common compulsion" can be seen to testify.

A Human Need

Freud sees religion as civilization's response to the hostility of which it is itself the object. Every individual, Freud tells us in *The Future of an Illusion,* "is virtually an enemy of civilization" (SE 21: 3). Civilization brings with it coercion and the renunciation of instinct. Yet this hostility also binds the individual to civilization, for civilization represents a protection against the superior powers of nature, on the one hand, and the "destructive . . . anti-social and anti-cultural" instincts of other human beings on the other (SE 21: 5). It is perhaps not a coincidence, therefore, that *The Future of an Illusion* is staged as a dialogue—that is, as an exemplary form of civilized hostility—between Freud and an "opponent" (*Gegner*) who speaks on behalf of religion and follows his every move with distrust and offers a series of critical remarks.

The discussion between Freud and Freud's opponent centers around the psychological need of human beings to humanize the impersonal forces and destinies that afflict them. Freud's opponent, the arch defender of human proclivities, immediately appeals to the natural predisposition of human beings to project their own existence into the world: "It is natural to them, something innate, as it were, to project their existence outwards into the world and to regard every event which they observe as the manifestation of beings who are at bottom like themselves" (SE 21: 22). Freud's opponent will then conclude that because self-projection is the "only method of comprehension" (SE 21: 22) that human beings have at their disposal, because human beings cannot understand the world except by measuring all that they observe by human measurements (by bringing everything back to themselves), they are therefore justified in doing so. In order to understand the world, according to Freud's opponent, human beings must defend against its nonhuman aspects.

Freud ends up expressing both his compassion for and his impatience before this all too human predicament. Thus, although Freud clearly recognizes the naturalness of the propensity of human beings "to personify everything they want to understand" (SE 21: 22), he also sees this propensity as a kind of neurotic infantilism when it is allowed to develop unchecked beyond a certain point. Just as the infant learns from the persons in its vicinity that the way to influence them is to establish a relationship with them, so too the adult learns to understand and to control everything it encounters by positing a common measure between itself and what it encounters. In this way, Freud contends, the adult recreates the parental house "in which [as a child, it] was so warm and comfortable [*in dem es ihm so warm und behaglich war*]" (SE 21: 49).

But surely, Freud cannot help but wonder, infantilism is meant to be surmounted:

> One cannot remain a child forever; one must in the end go out into "hostile life [*feindliche Leben*]." We may call this "*education to reality* [Erziehung zur Realität]." Need I confess to you that the sole purpose of my writing is to point out the necessity of this forward step? (SE 21: 49)

If, on the one hand, infantilism brings with it wish-fulfillment and consolation, on the other hand it comprises a system of illusions along with a "disavowal of reality [*Verleugnung der Wirklichkeit*]," such as we find in amentia, in a state of "blissful hallucinatory confusion" (SE 21: 43). Freud's irony is unmistakable here. Indeed, we would all prefer to keep so warm and comfortable.[3]

The longing for the parental home is for Freud a motive identical with the need for protection against all the undefined dangers that threaten the child in the external world. But when this defense against childish helplessness is carried on into adulthood, when the adult's reaction to helplessness acquires the "sanctity, rigidity and intolerance" of a religious system (SE 21: 51)—and the formation of religion is, for Freud, the adult's reaction to helplessness *par excellence*—it is time for civilization to give up its infantile wishes. Because the consolations of religion inevitably bring with them a "prohibition of thought" (SE 21: 51), it becomes imperative that civilization finally come of age. Civilization must grow up. Just as the individual must give up the warmth and comfort of the parental home, so must civilization give up the consolation of religious illusion and bear "the troubles of life and the cruelties of reality" (SE 21: 49).

Freud's conclusions are not without political and/or ethical implication. Not only does Freud not despair of humanity's ability to live without the wish-fulfilling and consolatory power of illusion, he sees the turn *away from* consolation (the consolations of religion) and *toward* reason as a step in the right direction—that is, in the direction of justice:

> By withdrawing their expectations from the other world and concentrating all their liberated energies on their earthly life [*auf das irdische Leben*], [human beings] will probably arrive at a state of things in which life will be more tolerable [*erträglich*] for everyone and civilization no longer oppressive to anyone. Then, with one of our fellow unbelievers [*mit einem unserer Unglaubensgenossen*], they will be able to say without regret:
>
> > Den Himmel überlassen wir [We leave heaven]
> > Den Engeln und den Spatzen [To the angels and the sparrows].
> > (SE 21: 50)

The energies directed toward the warmth and comforts of heaven will be withdrawn, detached from their object and thus liberated—made available—for other, worldly, applications. With human energies newly cathected on their life on earth, the heavens will be left to those creatures to whom they properly belong: to the angels and the sparrows as set forth in the two lines by Heine with which

Freud concludes his chapter. Not only religion but any doctrinal
system that takes on the psychological characteristics of religion
("the same sanctity, rigidity, and intolerance; the same prohibition
of thought" [SE 21: 51]) will have to be discarded in the end. These
systems must eventually be discarded in the name of what Freud
calls "the reality principle": that momentous step in the process of
human development when "what was presented in the mind was
no longer what was agreeable but what was real" (SE 12: 219). The
process of human development must finally dispel the consolatory
power of illusion that blinds us to reality: to that reality which we
would prefer not to see.

Religion, Freud tells us, is an illusion that derives its strength
from its readiness to fit in with our instinctual wishful impulses.
In the last of his *New Introductory Lectures on Psychoanalysis* (1933),
Freud describes religion as the attempt "to master the sensory world
in which we are situated by means of the wishful world [*mittels
der Wunschwelt*] which we have developed within us as a result of
biological and psychological necessities [*die wir infolge biologischer
und psychologischer Notwendigkeiten in uns entwickelt haben*]" (SE
22: 168). But the world is not a "nursery"; it is no "Kinderstube."

It is striking, however, that when Freud reiterates his critique of
religion in this lecture, he does so in very different terms: "Whatever
may be the value and importance of religion, it has *no right* in any
way to restrict thought [*sie hat* kein Recht, *das Denken irgendwie
zu beschränken*]—*no right*, therefore [*also auch* nicht das Recht],
to exclude itself from having thought applied to it" (SE 22: 170,
my emphasis). It would seem, in other words, that this infantilism
Freud calls "religion" not only claims a right it does not have but
also abuses the right of a legitimate claimant.

Religion's "prohibition against thought [*Denkverbot*]" presents
"a danger for the future of humanity [*eine Gefahr für die Zukunft
der Menschheit*]" because it is an abuser of rights (SE 22: 172).
Religion does not have the "right" to prohibit thought; it does
not have the "right" to stand outside of thought and exempt itself
from "having thought applied to it" (SE 22: 170). It does not have
the right because thought and thought alone—as opposed to the

recuperative humanization of nature—makes possible the maturation process of a civilization. The future of civilization itself, one might say, has a right to reality, as determined by objective principles of knowledge.

What is remarkable here is that Freud indicts religion's "Denkverbot" *in the name of the future*—and not, as was the case with his opponent, *in the name of the human*. Freud indicts religion in the name of the future, that is to say, in the name of a *right*, the right of reality to determine a future independent of our wishes and inclinations. But one should hasten to add that that in the name of which Freud issues his indictment stems not from any chance or anarchic future, but from a particular and quite special future, one that is bound up with a compulsion: "the common compulsion [*der gemeinsame Zwang*] exercised by . . . [the] dominance of reason [*Herrschaft der Vernunft*]" (SE 22: 171).

The grounds for Freud's indictment of religion are clear: only the common compulsion exercised by the dominance of reason can offer anything in the order of justice, that is to say, "a strong and uniting bond [*Band*] among human beings" (SE 22: 171). Only this common compulsion can lead the way to further unions. Only reason, the scientific spirit, the primacy of intellect are capable of gesturing beyond themselves, beyond the neurotic infantilism of human need—and to the future. The very notion of futurity for Freud is predicated on the dominance of reason but more particularly on the exercise of a "common compulsion." Could it be, then, that there is something about the nature of reason that "stands surety [*bürgt*]" for the future of "a strong and uniting bond among human beings" (SE 22: 171)? Is there something in reason itself that would be the ground not only of Freud's "common compulsion" but also of the alternative future of the Enlightenment?

The Need of Reason

To read this future of the Enlightenment, however, we must first return to Kant. Kant will conclude his 1786 essay "What Is Orientation in Thinking?" with an impassioned appeal to the future:

Friends of the human race and of all that it holds most holy! [*Freunde des Menschengeschlechts und dessen, was ihm am heiligsten ist*!] Accept whatever seems most credible to you after careful and honest examination ... but do not deny reason that prerogative which makes it the greatest good on earth, namely its right to be the ultimate touchstone of truth [*streitet der Vernunft nicht das, was sie zum höchsten Gut auf Erden macht, nämlich das Vorrecht ab, der letzte Probierstein der Wahrheit zu sein*]. (DO 146; 249)

What is at stake for Kant in this essay—just as it was for Freud in *The Future of an Illusion*—is the prerogative or right (*Vor-recht*) of reason to be the final arbiter of truth, the supreme touchstone of the reliability of a judgment. For Kant, however, this right is first a privilege (*Vorrecht*) and as privilege it must never be abused.

The good of the world (*das Weltbeste*) depends on the free and unfettered use of reason. Freedom of thought, says Kant, must remain "inviolate [*ungekränkt*]" if human beings are not to fall prey to zealotry, superstition, and the political repressions that inevitably follow from them (DO 144; 247). Kant sees civil coercion (*bürgerliche Zwang*) and moral constraint (*Gewissenszwang*) as the most conspicuous forms of opposition to freedom of thought. However, Kant will also point to a third form of opposition—to what is perhaps the most formidable form of opposition since it comes from within reason itself. For Freud, the best hope for the future "is that intellect—the scientific spirit, reason—may in process of time establish a dictatorship in the mental life of man" (SE 22: 171). For Kant, on the contrary, the "dictatorship" or despotism of speculative reason represents a third form of opposition to freedom of thought.

Freedom of thought signifies for Kant the subjection of reason to no laws other than those which reason imposes on itself. Thus, in addition to civil coercion and moral constraint, opposition to freedom of thought may come from "the maxim of the *lawless use* of reason [*die Maxime eines* gesetzlosen Gebrauchs *der Vernunft*]" (DO 145; 247): that is, from the emancipation of reason from its own restrictions. When reason acquires a "presumptuous confidence in the independence of its own powers from every restriction" (DO 146; 248), it quickly degenerates into misuse. The result is a conviction in the absolute and exclusive authority of speculative reason ("intellect . . . the scientific spirit, reason"). One might say that in such cases speculative reason itself becomes a religion or dictatorship of sorts—"accept[ing] only what can be justified on *objective* grounds and by dogmatic conviction . . . brashly dismiss[ing] everything else" (DO 146; 248).

The consequences of this presumed independence are very serious indeed, for, as Kant demonstrates, they lead first to "the attitude known as *libertinism* [Freigesterei] (i.e. the principle of no longer acknowledging any duty)" and finally to the abolition of freedom of thought altogether (DO 146; 249). In the end, freedom of thought destroys itself "when it wills to proceed independently of the very laws of reason [*wenn sie so gar unabhängig von Gesetzen der Vernunft verfahren will*]" (DO 146; 249). The laws of reason impose restrictions on the powers of reason, and reason depends upon these laws—it *needs* these laws—for its proper use. Hence, the lawless use of reason is also said to stem from "the maxim of the independence of reason from its *own need* [*von ihrem* eigenen Bedürfnis])" (DO 146; 249).

Now Kant's notion of "orientation in thinking" arises precisely in connection with this need. Orientation in thinking is the means whereby pure reason regulates its use "when, taking leave of known objects (of experience), it seeks to extend its sphere beyond the frontiers of experience and no longer encounters any objects of intuition whatsoever" (DO 136; 239–40). Just as we are able to orient ourselves in space (i.e. mathematically) so too, Kant contends, are we able to orient ourselves in thought (i.e. logically). To orient oneself in thought is to be guided by a subjective principle of reason where objective principles of reason are lacking:

This subjective means which still remains available to [reason] is simply the feeling of a *need* which is inherent in reason itself [*Dies subjektive Mittel, das alsdann noch übrig bleibt, ist kein anderes als das Gefühl des der Vernunft eigenen* Bedürfnisses]. (DO 136; 239–40)

When pure reason is no longer in a position to subsume its judgments under specific maxims according to objective principles, it finds guidance in a subjective principle. This subjective principle, or that which is left over ("übrig bleibt") when the natural data of reason and experience are insufficient is, says Kant, "simply the feeling of a *need*"—indeed, a need that is "inherent in reason itself."

Reason needs to find subjective means of satisfying itself when it cannot be satisfied in any other way, for "reason must sooner or later be satisfied [*die Vernunft will einmal befriedigt sein*]" (DO 136; 240). Reason must be satisfied because, as Kant makes clear, there must be (moral) judgment. Reason must pass judgment. It is not a question, in other words, of whether or not we wish to judge; judgment in this case is not a "voluntary [*willkürlich*]" matter. Rather, and Kant is very explicit here: at issue is the problem of judgment where, on the one hand, judgment is made "*necessary* by a real need (in fact by a need which reason imposes on itself)" and, on the other, *impossible* because of a "lack of knowledge in respect of factors essential to the judgment [*wo . . . Mangel des Wissens in Ansehung der zum Urteil erforderlichen Stücke uns einschränkt*]" (DO 136; 240, my emphasis). When reason is compelled (*genötigt*) to pass judgment but lacks the objective grounds for doing so, it is justified in appealing to subjective grounds, in light of which judgment can be passed.

Kant draws a fundamental distinction here between the *need* of reason in its speculative use (our need to make the concept of the unlimited the basis of the concept of all contingent things) and the *need* of reason in its practical use (our need to assume that the unlimited exists because we must pass moral judgment). In its speculative use, the need of reason is merely "conditional," for it depends on whether or not we *wish to pass judgment*. "Much more important, however," says Kant, "is the need of reason in its practical use, because this is unconditional [*unbedingt*]" (DO 139; 242). The use of practical reason is unconditional because we are "compelled [*genötigt werden*]" to assume something—the existence of the unlimited—"not only if we *wish* to pass judgment [as would be the case of the need of reason in its speculative use], but because we *must pass judgment* [*nicht bloß . . . wenn wir* urteilen

wollen, *sondern weil wir* urteilen müssen]" (DO 139; 242). Reason
needs to assume the existence of the unlimited because it needs
to give objective (practical) reality to the moral law. We must pass
judgment: that is, we must formulate moral laws (DO 139; 242).

And what is more, this tension—the tension that arises between
the impossibility of judging according to objective principles of
reason, on the one hand, and the irreducible necessity of arriving at
judgment, on the other—gives way to one of the strangest assertion
of "right" in Kant's work:

> It is at this point ... that *the right of the need* of reason [das Recht
> des Bedürfnisses *der Vernunft*] supervenes as a subjective ground for
> presupposing and accepting something which reason cannot presume
> to know on objective grounds, and hence for *orienting* ourselves in
> thought—i.e. in the immeasurable space of the supra-sensory realm
> which we see as full of utter darkness—purely by means of the need
> of reason itself [*lediglich durch ihr eigenes Bedürfnis zu* orientieren].
> (DO 137; 241)

The need of reason gives reason the right "*to presuppose* [vorauszuset-
zen]" the real possibility of something that can never be attested to
by experience (DO 141; 244). Kant will call this subjective source of
judgment "rational belief" (*Vernunftglaube*) because it is based on
no other data than those that are inherent in pure reason. Not only
does reason need to presuppose something it can understand, it is
also justified in doing so, says Kant. Need alone, in other words,
gives reason the right to extend the notion of right to a subjective
principle of thought. The end result is that need and right become
indistinguishable here. And it is precisely at this point where need
and right become indistinguishable that we see speculative reason
at risk of venturing beyond its proper limits.

Let us recall, however, that this blurring of concepts takes place
at the limits of speculative reason, which is to say, at the limits of
sensibility. Need and right become indistinguishable, that is, when
it is a matter of "the *self-preservation* of reason [Selbsterhaltung
der Vernunft]" (DO 147n; 249n). When reason is compelled to
pass judgment but lacks the objective grounds for doing so, it
must appeal to subjective grounds because it has an essential need,

"a necessary need [*ein notwendiges Bedürfnis*]" (DO 141; 244), to ground its judgment. It is no accident, furthermore, that the notion of "self-preservation"—along with that of orientation in thinking—appear at a moment when speculative reason threatens to supplant reason in its pure (practical) employment.

When (pure) reason "perceives its own deficiency [*sieht ihren Mangel ein*]," says Kant—its incapacity to know on objective grounds—it "produces a feeling of need through the *cognitive drive* [*wirkt durch den* Erkenntnistrieb *das Gefühl des Bedürfnisses*]" (DO 139n; 243n). Reason produces a feeling through a drive. The grammar of this sentence is perfectly clear: we have an active verb, of which "reason" is the subject and "feeling" the direct object. What is less clear, however, is the function of the prepositional phrase introduced by "through." How exactly are we to read "through" here? How are we to understand, to read through "through" ("*durch*" *durchlesen*)? What is the relation of the drive to the feeling? Is the drive more than, other than, independent of the feeling? Does the cognitive drive serve the feeling; is the drive merely a convenient means of expressing the feeling? Or is the drive the whole of the feeling, the feeling as drive? Would the cognitive drive be a translation of sorts, produced by reason because reason needs specific grounds for its satisfaction? Or is the cognitive drive *the* feeling of need, the feeling of need *par excellence* produced by reason because reason finds itself in an intolerable position? Is the feeling of need a strategy or a crisis? We cannot know. All we know is that reason does not feel: "Die Vernunft fühlt nicht" (DO 139n; 243n). That is to say, reason is not what we would call "human reason"; or rather what is human in reason is but the life (of the cognitive) drive.

What Kant does tell us—in a footnote—is that the feeling of need, which is inherent in reason, is related to moral feeling: "Es ist hiemit wie mit dem moralischen Gefühl bewandt" (DO 139n; 243n). Thus, even though it is a feeling, it is not a feeling received through any outside influence; it is a feeling produced by reason alone. In the case of moral feeling, of course, the very feeling that promotes the influence of the moral law is "produced or occasioned [*verursacht oder gewirkt*]" (DO 139n; 243n) by moral laws, that is, by pure practical reason. Moral law, which "has its source entirely in reason [*entspringt gänzlich aus der Vernunft*]" (DO 139n; 243n) is the cause of moral feeling.

In the case of moral feeling, reason produces a feeling "because the active yet free will needs specific grounds [on which to act: *indem der rege und doch freie Wille bestimmter Gründe bedarf*]" (DO 139n; 243n). The moral law is not only a formal determining ground of action through pure practical reason, it is also a subjective ground of determination for sensuous and finite beings (i.e., imperfectly rational beings). But how does this apply in the case of reason's feeling of need? Why does reason produce a feeling of need through the cognitive drive? Moral feeling, as we have seen, is the effect of moral law upon an imperfectly rational subject, a subject whose will does not in itself completely accord with reason.[4] Moral feeling is the space that separates objective necessity (moral law) from subjective contingency (human motivation). In the case of the need of reason, however, why must there be feeling?

Reason "perceives its own deficiencies [*sieht ihren Mangel ein*]," says Kant, and "effects [*wirkt*] a feeling of need through the cognitive drive" (DO 139n; 243n). However we are to understand this statement, the cognitive drive, it would seem, carries on a twofold existence: on the one hand, it serves to define and distinguish the human, marking thus the specificity of the human (as the *res cogitans, the animal rationale*). On the other hand, it conveys a feeling of need: a feeling that is inaccessible to it and yet communicable *through* it. Given the kinship of the feeling of need with moral feeling, moreover, the feeling of need might best be described as the cognitive categorical imperative, an "intellectual categorical imperative"[5] that commands us always to seek further conditions: You must always seek further! In other words, the need of reason prohibits a limitation on thinking, and the cognitive drive is the sign (or symptom) of this prohibition.

And yet, as we will see, this passage from the principles of speculative reason to the principles of practical reason gives rise to something new: the subordination of speculative reason to practical reason, on the one hand, and a language of power, on the other.

Passing On

When in *The Interpretation of Dreams* Freud tells us that rational thought is a "substitute for hallucinatory desire" (SE 5: 567), it is because hallucinatory wish fulfillment has the same goal as rational thinking. Rational systems, Freud explains, substitute for hallucinatory wish fulfillment because they appeal to the same general principle. Both strive to reduce tension by identificatory appropriation, that is, by assimilating differences to themselves. Speculative thinking and narcissism, Freud tells us, are never completely separable.

Speculative thinking, Kant tells us in the Preface to the second edition of the *Critique of Pure Reason*, must never venture beyond the limits of experience because the principles with which it ventures out do not extend the use of reason but rather, "as we find on closer scrutiny, inevitably *narrow* it" (B xxiv). Speculative reason must not fall prey to pathological narcissism. Indeed, as we have seen, if the principles with which it ventures out beyond experience—principles that belong to sensibility and extend only to objects of possible experience—are applied to what cannot be an object of experience, they "always change [the latter] into an appearance, thus rendering all *practical extension* of pure reason impossible" (B xxx). The narcissism of speculative reason must be checked, in other words, if the real—that is, the moral here—is not to be limited to the bounds of human sensibility.

But how are we to understand the narcissistic tendencies of speculative reason in the first place? Why this tendency on the part of speculative reason to do away with practical reason? What exactly is the threat of the "practical" here? For this, however, we must turn to the *Critique of Practical Reason*:

> It is a question [*so ist die Frage*] of whether speculative reason, which knows nothing of that which the practical reason offers for its acceptance, must take up these principles and seek to integrate them, even though they exceed it, with its own concepts, as a foreign possession handed over to it [*ob spekulative Vernunft . . . diese Sätze aufnehmen und sie, ob sie gleich für sie überschwenglich sind, mit ihren Begriffen als*

einen fremden, auf sie übertragenen Besitz zu vereinigen suchen müsse]; or whether it is justified in stubbornly following its own isolated interest, rejecting, according to the canon of Epicurus, everything as an empty sophism [*alles als leere Vernünftelei*] which does not certify its objective reality by manifest examples from experience, doing so however much it is interwoven with the interest of the practical (pure) use of reason [*wenn es gleich noch so sehr mit dem Interesse des praktischen (reinen) Gebrauchs verwebt*] and however far removed from contradicting the theoretical, merely because it infringes [*Abbruch tut*] upon the interest of the speculative reason by removing the bounds which the latter has set itself, exposing it to every nonsense and delusion of the imagination [*daß es die Grenzen, die diese sich selbst gesetzt, aufhebt und sie allem Unsinn oder Wahnsinn der Einbildungskraft preisgibt*]. (KprV 120; 125)

What is at issue in the association of pure practical reason with speculative reason is primacy—the primacy of pure practical over speculative reason. But this is also a theoretical question for Kant: How is speculative reason to integrate or appropriate that which exceeds it? How is speculative reason to take in something that dislocates it and leaves it vulnerable (*preisgibt*) to the unbridled fantasy of the imagination? How is speculative reason even to begin to take up (*aufnehmen*), to take into itself anything at all—let alone a principle that exceeds it—when the limits, the boundaries it has set itself have been *demolished*?

Kant's answer is uncompromising: speculative reason must accept the propositions that belong inseparably (*unabtrennlich*) to the practical interest of pure reason—

It must assume them indeed as something offered from the outside and not grown in its own soil [*zwar als ein ihr fremdes Angebot, das nicht auf ihrem Boden erwachsen... ist*], and it must seek to compare and connect them [*zu vergleichen und zu verknüpfen suchen*] with everything which it has in its power as speculative reason. It must remember that they are not its own insights but extensions of its use in some other respect, viz., the practical; and that this is not in the least opposed to its interest, which lies in the restriction of speculative folly. (KprV 121; 126)

Speculative reason must do two contradictory things, and it must do them simultaneously: it must preserve the foreignness of the possession that has been handed over to it and it must remain itself. It must neither reduce the foreign to itself (which would be an act of appropriation) nor let itself be reduced to the foreign (an act of expropriation). Foreign possessions are not possessions in the usual sense—"they are not its own insights" says Kant—but neither are these foreign possessions "in the least opposed" to the interest of speculative reason.[6]

Thus, the relation of speculative reason to practical reason is not one of opposition. This is the case because "pure practical reason" and "speculative reason" are not symmetrical terms; rather practical reason has primacy over speculative reason. Indeed,

> [w]ithout this subordination [*Unterordnung*], a conflict of reason with itself would arise, since if the speculative and the practical reason were simply arranged side by side (coordinated) [*wenn sie einander bloß beigeordnet (koordiniert) wären*], the first would close its borders [*Grenze*] and admit into its domain [*Gebiet*] nothing from the latter, while the latter would extend its boundaries [*Grenzen*] over everything, and, when its needs required [*wo es ihr Bedürfnis erheischt*], would seek to comprehend the former within them. (KprV 121; 126).

Were it not for the subordination of speculative reason to practical reason, there would be no possibility of possession that was not either an appropriation (ad-proprius) or an expropriation (ex-proprius), the one opposing the other (ad versus ex). Were it not for this asymmetry, the exappropriation of speculative reason would not be possible, would not remain the only hope for the *real* possibility of practical sources of knowledge.

The need of reason is thus not a negation of speculative reason. On the contrary, the right of the need of reason arises from reason's failure to ground itself, as speculative reason, on objective principles of knowledge (i.e. principles internal to its system). Reason needs this cognitive failure in order to be itself—that is, not only speculative but also practical. One might say that "practical reason" speaks the language of speculative reason, but it does so as a foreigner, that is, from a place that is irreducible to the self-identity or closure of speculative reason. Speculative reason must always strive and fail to assimilate what is offered it "from the outside." If this assimilation is not possible—and it must not be possible or achievable for speculative reason to be what it is—it is certainly not because of a boundary that comes to close off a given space. For such spaces or realms would be homogeneous with one another, symmetrical and commensurable on either side of a dividing line. Rather it would be because of another organization of space altogether in which the "outside" remains forever outside, heterogeneous to every "inside" and thus also to the faculty of human understanding. An "outside" that would be thus literally "unacceptable" to speculative reason and whose demand to be "taken up" could only be passed on as intellectual imperative, that is, as a feeling of need.

Theoretical reason is not thereby extended in its knowledge of objects. However, as Kant suggests, it is extended in its knowledge of reason in general:

> It [is] therefore no extension [*Erweiterung*] of knowledge of given supersensuous objects, but still an extension of theoretical reason and of its knowledge with respect to the supersensuous in general, inasmuch as knowledge is compelled [*genötigt*] to concede that there are such objects without more exactly defining them. (KprV 135–36; 140–41)

Theoretical reason is forced to accept the real possibility of something it can never grasp; it is compelled, forced by another power to do what it would prefer not to do. What is more, the extension in question has a dampening effect on human reason's "presumptuous confidence in the independence of its own powers" (DO 146; 248), that is to say, on the narcissism of human reason. Indeed this extension is not the end of the story. Instead, as Kant says, once reason is "in possession of this accession [*im Besitze dieses Zuwachses*]," for the security of its practical employment it sets to work "as speculative reason" purifying its concepts "in order to ward off anthropomorphism [*Anthropomorphismus*]...and fanaticism [*Fanatizismus*]" (DO 135–36; 141). When reason goes back to work (*zu Werke gehen*) as speculative reason, what does it do? It analyzes the dangers of anthropomorphism (recuperative humanization) and the dogmatic pretensions of religion.

In conclusion, one would have to say that the legacy of the Enlightenment has at least as much to do with a "common compulsion" and a "need" of reason as it does with the voice of intellect. In this context, we can also see that the concept of reason is always accompanied by what can only be described as a language of power. For Freud, our best hope is that intellect—"or let us call it by the name that is familiar to us, reason"—may in time establish "a *dictatorship* in the mental life of man" (SE 22: 171, my emphasis). The powers of reason must dispel the illusions of religion in order to lay the foundation of a new community—a community bound by reason. However, as we have seen, a community bound by reason—indeed civilization itself—creates a "bond" (*Band*) among human beings by "binding" (*binden*) the hetero-aggression to which human beings are by nature predisposed. Thus, a strong and uniting *bond* (Band) among human beings depends on the reversal of what was at first a destructive and violent impulse: "[S]ocial feeling is based upon the reversal of what was first a hostile feeling into a positively-toned bond [*eine positiv betonte Bindung*] of the nature of an identification" (SE 18: 153). A community bound by reason owes its binding force, in other words, to an energy that—unbound—would "murder even for trifles" (SE 14: 297).

For Kant, not only can speculative reason not close its borders to the principles of practical reason, it must keep them open at all costs—even if it means exposing itself "to every nonsense and delusion of the imagination." Speculative reason is compelled by the superior powers of practical reason to admit into its domain principles that not only exceed it but fracture, wound, and traumatize its interiority. Indeed, everything changes from the moment words like "subordination," "compulsion," "vulnerability" enter the scene, that is, from the moment reason emerges as a language of power (unconditional necessity) from a language of cognition.[7] And might it not be the case, in the end, that it is this new emergence, this latest "Ausgang," that bears both the mark and the seal of the Enlightenment?

§ 1 The Legacy of the Future

Kant and the Ethical Question

Ne pas avoir choisi sa liberté—voilà la suprême absurdité et le
suprême tragique de l'existence, voilà l'irrationnel.

— (Emmanuel Levinas, *Totalité et Infini*)

Invitation

There is a much noted strangeness about Kant's invocation of
Copernicus in support of his own revolutionary turn in the Preface
to the second edition of the *Critique of Pure Reason*.[1] The reference to Copernicus is strange, so it is argued, because of what
appears to be Kant's anthropocentric (or geocentric) fallacy.[2] As
Freud makes clear in another revolutionary context, the name and
work of Copernicus signify for us the end of an illusion; they mark,
in Freud's language, the final and decisive break with the narcissistic presumption of the earth's central and stationary position in
the universe.[3] Troubling and strangely incomprehensible, therefore, becomes Kant's appeal to a radical decentering of the universe
when his own analogy is made in view of a no less radical, transcendental recentering of human knowledge in its a priori conditions of
possibility. Missing from Kant's revolutionary perspective, it would
seem, is the cosmological turn of Copernicus. Transcendental idealism would not be a Copernican change in point of view, in other
words, because its orientation remains abidingly human.

But perhaps the trouble lies in our not being troubled enough.
Perhaps, on the contrary, it is we who should be more cautious,
more tentative in our judgment, more distrusting of our senses
when an essential feature of Copernicus's "change in point of view

[*Umänderung der Denkart*]" (B xxii) is its capacity to venture forth *against* the senses—"auf eine widersinnische... Art" (B xxii).[4] Can we be so certain, in other words—given our natural tendency to laziness and inertia (indeed to narcissism)[5] –that we, like those thinkers who "entangle themselves to the point of absurdity in Tychonic cycles and epicycles" (SF 149; 83), have not remained fixed in our "way of explaining appearances" and in our original "Standpunkt" (SF 149; 83)? Could it not be that like these thinkers—"otherwise not unwise" (SF 149; 83)—we too have obstinately refused to assume the implications of a radical change of perspective, that we too have missed the revolution?

What if Kant's most revolutionary turn were not to be located in his *Critique of Pure Reason*? What if, furthermore, this revolutionary turn were the one in which we were not only implicated but newly implicated? What if, in other words, *we* played a necessary role in the emergence of what is distinctly Kantian about this revolution? What if we were not simply the passive recipients but also the acting heirs—a passivity that would not be incompatible with freedom and autonomy—of a legacy that was itself radically ethical in nature? Such, I will suggest, is the properly Kantian (Copernican) revolution: a turn that is no longer an attempt, even a revolutionary one, to make possible (or conceivable) that which was formerly impossible (or inconceivable) but rather *a shift in the notion of possibility itself.* This shift introduces, I will argue, a condition of possibility that is distinct *and* inseparable from an epistemological condition of possibility, on the one hand, and from a practical condition of possibility on the other. For what we will see emerge is a passage (which has nothing to do with the aesthetic), the irreversible passage from speculative "sources of cognition [*Erkenntnisquellen*]" (B xxvi) to non-speculative or practical "sources of cognition"—a passage or transition that belongs thus to neither realm exclusively. As such, it is a passage that is neither theoretical nor practical (it is not practical reason itself because practical reason exists independently of any critical or epistemological examination of it: indeed it is found in the most ordinary human reason according to Kant); rather it is equally poised between both.

Furthermore, it is to such a possibility of passage, I will claim, that *we* are called on to respond.[6] We are "summoned [*aufgefordert*]" (B xxi), in other words, against the very nature of our representations, "auf eine widersinnische, aber doch wahre Art" (B xxii), against the very modality of possibility; we are being called *per impossibile* to a possibility beyond theoretical and practical possibility, which, it will turn out, is nothing less than the possibility of the future. Like the "invisible, world-binding force" (B xxii, modified) of the Newtonian attraction that "would have remained forever undiscovered" (B xxii) had it not been for Copernicus's daring hypothesis—Kant's revolution opens a space for future revolutions. But it does something more as well: and it is "this something more [*dieses Mehrere*]" (B xxvi) that makes the space left "empty [*leer*]" (B xxi) by speculative reason not a blank but already a bequest and thus already the possibility of the step beyond.

Thus, besides the perhaps inescapable risk of oedipal overzealousness in accusing Kant of an anthropocentric "fallacy"—a rather minor risk if one is to judge by the unrestrained tones of his accusers—there lies, I will suggest, the risk of skirting an ethical revolution (a revolution that takes place without violence, without hostility) whose emergence on the scene may bespeak an anthropotropism far more revolutionary[7] and decentering than what has yet been understood under the name "Kant."

Laying the Groundwork

THE THREAT OF HETERONOMY

In the Second Section of the *Grounding for the Metaphysics of Morals*, written in 1785, one finds an argument structured very closely along the lines of the turn that Kant will later associate with the name Copernicus. In the same way that it is impossible in the epistemological realm to explain the possibility of a priori knowledge if one assumes that knowledge must conform to objects, "so too, in the practical context, one cannot explain the possibility of a categorical imperative, or more generally, an a priori practical principle with the requisite universality and necessity"[8] if one continues to assume that an object of the will is the source of moral requirements.

> In every case where an object of the will [*ein Objekt des Willens*] must be laid down as the grounds [*zum Grunde gelegt werden muß*] for prescribing a rule to determine the will, there the rule is nothing but heteronomy; the imperative is conditioned, viz.: *if* or *because* one wills this object, one should act thus or thus; hence the imperative can never command morally, i.e. categorically. (Gr 444; 47)

If the will goes outside of itself and seeks the law of its determination "in the property [*Beschaffenheit*] of any of its objects [*Objekte*]" (Gr 441; 45) then heteronomy is always the result. Heteronomy is the result when the will is determined by any "foreign impulse [*fremder Antrieb*]" (Gr 444; 47) whatsoever, whether this foreign impulse determines the will by means of sensibility or by means of reason directed to objects of our possible volition (e.g. the pursuit of perfection).

Autonomy of the will, on the other hand, is introduced in the *Grundlegung* as the necessary condition of the possibility of moral law. In the case of a finite rational being, the defining characteristic of autonomy of the will is not an independence from *causal* determination by alien sources—our needs or desires as sensuous beings—since such independence (which Kant calls "negative freedom") is already presupposed by Kant's notion of practical spontaneity and by the very concept of an *arbitrium liberum*. Rather it is a "motivational independence, that is, a capacity for self-determination independently of, and even contrary to these needs."[9] Kant identifies autonomy with "the property [*Beschaffenheit*] that the will has of being a law to itself (independently of any property of the objects of volition [*Gegenstände des Wollens*])" (Gr 440; 44). Only if the will possesses this property, only if the will is its own supreme lawgiver, can one account for the possibility of something other than a conditioned or hypothetical imperative. The principle of autonomy, "das alleinige Prinzip der Moral" (Gr 440), is, consequently, the expression of the requirement to act on the basis of this property. As principle, autonomy demands that one act from a self-determined, desire-independent motive (for imperfectly rational beings who are constitutionally susceptible to self-deception, this expression must take the form of a command, namely the categorical imperative). The supreme principle of morality enjoins all rational beings with a will to choose maxims that are suitable as universal laws not because of some outside interest or desire but rather *because* of their very suitability for universal law. An unconditioned practical principle knows no restrictions; it contains only the necessity that universalizability function as the ultimate standard governing all choice of maxims. Thus, on the one hand, a universally and unconditionally valid practical law must be formal in the sense that it must abstract from any material object of the will; on the other hand, it requires that a maxim be adopted solely for its legislative form, i.e. its universalizability. Autonomy of the will is therefore both the necessary condition of the possibility of the moral law (it must be a property of the will) and the expression of this possibility as law (it is the principle of morality).

But a necessity "that is unconditioned and . . . objective and hence universally valid" (Gr 416; 26) such as the moral law requires cannot be derived from the particular constitution of human beings. For no example drawn from human experience can testify to a will that has been determined solely by universal law without other incentive or desire (such may appear to be the case, of course, but, as Kant reminds us, the possibilities of self-deception are infinite and imperceptible). Indeed the threat of heteronomy is so great for human beings and one's human allegiance to the "dear self [*das liebe Selbst*]" (Gr 407; 20) so ineradicable that the world has perhaps never seen an example of a moral action that "would have sprung [*entsprungen wäre*]" (Gr 408; 20) from pure and unmixed sources.

And the threat of heteronomy is greater still, for, as Kant declares, the principle of heteronomy is the bane of all moral theories. Not only are morals "liable to all kinds of corruption" (Gr 390; 3), but moral philosophy itself risks confusing pure principles with impure ones and thus "spoil[ing]. . . the purity of morals and counteract[ing] its own end" (Gr 390; 3). When moral philosophy does not begin with pure philosophy (metaphysics), when moral philosophy does not begin by purifying its principles of the very conditions of human desire[10]—conditions that can only be known a posteriori—then "there can be no moral philosophy at all" (Gr 390; 3), that is, no moral philosophy that could give account of the objective necessity (non-anthropological, non-theological) of moral law. As sensuous beings, we have a natural "propensity [*Hang*]" to quibble with the strict laws of duty and to make them, wherever possible, "more compatible with our wishes and inclinations" (Gr 405; 17). But when the language of desire (inclination, taste) permeates so much of our contemporary literature on Kant—whether it be in terms of making Kant's moral philosophy more "palatable" or less "repugnant" in the tradition of Schiller, or dismissing it as "unsatisfying" in the tradition of Hegel[11]—it becomes not only timely but *urgent* to raise the question of Kant's formalism once again. Is it possible that, in the name of our palate and our sensibility, in the name of heteronomy itself, Kant's defenders and prosecutors alike have in fact, right from the start, "corrupted" the moral law in its foundation and destroyed its "dignity [*Würde*]" (Gr 405; 17)? For, as we all know—and the practical threat is very real today in academic philosophy—it is certainly bad for the business of moral philosophy when it does not give us what we want.

Indeed Kant's formalism has inspired such resistance that one begins to suspect that it is formalism itself that must be banished from our midst (like Coriolanus), no matter how rigorous and enriching its analytic powers.[12] In the wake of Kant's categorical imperative, how many a well-intentioned moral theory has arisen whose aim is always to bring the abstract, formal structures of philosophy into a harmonious expression with their concrete, *human*, and worldly effects?[13] And yet, as Kant warns us repeatedly, theories based on human inclination or desire can produce only monstrosities. Such theories leave us not with morality at all but, much to our horror and surprise, with "some ill-begotten bastard patched up from limbs of quite varied ancestry [*einen aus Gliedern ganz verschiedener Abstammung zusammengeflickten Bastard*]"

(Gr 426; 34). The defenders of Kant who fear the great philosopher may have forsaken or betrayed the world by being too formalistic may be assuming all too readily that when we refer to something called "the human" we know what it is we are talking about, even though there is probably no word whose changing definition in this century has proved more abusive and lethal than "the human." One might conclude, justifiably, that these critics, on the contrary, have not been "nearly formalistic enough."[14] Philosophy, Kant tells us, is not empirical psychology. In their disavowal of the most formalistic aspects of his moral philosophy, in their appeals to our "moral intuition," Kant's greatest apologists may have unwittingly unleashed on the moral scene a psychology (and a politics) that is anything but Kantian. What I will suggest in this chapter, on the contrary, is that it is precisely Kant's formalism that leaves us with the most radical form of resistance, a resistance whose traces hinder (for better or for worse) any ideological closure of the "human," a resistance whose legacy can only be called the "future."[15]

ABSOLUTE HETERONOMY

All laws determined by reference to an "object [*Objekt*]," says Kant, yield heteronomy. In such cases, as we have seen, the will "does not give itself the law, but the object does so because of its *relation* [Verhältnis] to the will" (Gr 441; 45, my emphasis). "Object," here, refers to an object of practical reason, which is to say, any "possible state of affairs regarded by an agent as in some sense good."[16] This relation may rest on inclination (the pursuit of happiness) or it may rest on representations of reason (the pursuit of perfection), but in both cases the will admits only of hypothetical imperatives: "I ought to do something because I will something else" (Gr 441; 45). The determining ground of the will in a heteronomous model of volition is thus extrinsic to the will: some contingent (hypothetical) and material end enters into the practical rule as its condition of possibility. A fundamental opposition between autonomy and heteronomy of the will—between moral theories committed to the former principle and eudemonic theories committed to the latter— saturates and structures the entire realm of the practical according to

Kant. Either the will gives itself the law and we choose maxims that are universalizable because of their legislative form, in which case we have autonomy, or the law is pathological and given to the will from without, in which case we have heteronomy—rules of skill, counsels of prudence but nothing that could be called a *moral* law.

The principle of autonomy involves a very different kind of "relation [*Verhältnis*]," a relation that is not, as in the case of heteronomy, the will's relation to a thing or to a state of affairs. Rather the will's relation is a relation to itself, a relation of self-determination: it is "the relation of a will to itself [*das Verhältnis eines Willens zu sich selbst*] insofar as it is determined solely by reason" (Gr 427; 35). Given that the faculty of self-determination (i.e. the relation of a will of a rational being to the will of a rational being) is to be found in all rational beings with a will by definition, the will's relation of self-determination is also by extension a relation of self-determination to self-determination, that is to say, the relation of the will of one rational being to the will of another rational being.

> The practical necessity of acting according to ... duty ... does not rest on feelings, impulses, and inclinations, *but only on the relation of rational beings to one another* [sondern bloß auf dem Verhältnisse vernünftiger Wesen zueinander], a relation in which the will of a rational being must always be regarded at the same time as *law-giving* [*jederzeit zugleich als* gesetzgebend] ... as an *end in itself.* (Gr 434; 40[17])

Indeed the relation of rational beings to rational beings is incommensurable with the relation of rational beings to objects of practical reason. The categorical imperative, the supreme principle of practical necessitation for human beings, is the expression of this incommensurability. For an absolute distinction must be drawn between "beings [*Wesen*]" that have only a relative value as means and "are therefore called *things* [*und heißen daher* Sachen]," and beings that are "rational [*vernünftige*]" and are called "*persons* [Personen *genannt werden*]" insofar as "their nature already marks them out as ends in themselves, i.e., as something which is not to be used merely as means" (Gr 428; 36). A limit is thereby set on the arbitrary use of rational beings. A rational being is "an object of respect [*ein*

Gegenstand der Achtung]" (Gr 428; 36), and its existence has in it-self an absolute worth. Otherwise, says Kant—and this is quite an otherwise for it holds the very possibility of moral law is its sway—"no supreme practical principle could be found for reason at all" (Gr 428; 36).[18] If there is to be a supreme practical principle, if there is to be absolute necessity and moral law—and therefore a moral command or a categorical imperative for imperfectly rational beings such as ourselves—then there must be "something [*etwas*]" whose value is not conditioned and hence contingent, "something whose existence has in itself an absolute worth, something which as an end in itself could be a ground of determinate laws" (Gr 428; 35). There must be something, an "independently existing end [*selbständiger Zweck*]" that "cannot be subordinated [*nachgesetzt werden*]" (Gr 437; 42) to any other object, an end that is objective and necessary, for without such an end morality would remain "a mere phantom [*bloßes Hirngespinst*] of human imagination" (Gr 407; 19), a vaporous "dream [*Traum*] of sweet illusions" (Gr 426; 34).

"Now I say," Kant will say, "that a human being, and in general every rational being, exists as an end in itself" (Gr 428; 35). But he says more: "rational nature [*die vernünftige Natur*] exists as an end in itself" (Gr 429; 36). Indeed, Kant will insist on strict universality:

"Thou shalt not lie," does not hold merely for human beings [*Menschen*], as if other rational beings [*andere vernünftige Wesen*] did not have to abide by it. (Gr 389; 2)

[U]nless we want to deny the concept of morality all truth and all reference to a possible object, we cannot but admit that the moral law is of such widespread significance that it must hold not merely for human beings [*Menschen*] but for *all rational beings generally* [alle vernünftigen Wesen überhaupt], and that it must be valid not merely under contingent conditions and with exceptions but must be absolutely necessary. (Gr 408; 20)

[Pure practical] principles should not be made dependent on the particular nature of human reason [*von der besonderen Natur der menschlichen Vernunft*], as speculative philosophy may permit and even sometimes find necessary; but, rather, the principles should be derived from the universal concept of a rational being in general [*aus dem allgemeinen Begriffe eines vernünftigen Wesens überhaupt*]. (Gr 412; 23)

For the universality with which [moral] laws ought to hold for all rational beings without exception (the unconditioned practical necessity imposed by moral laws on such beings) falls away if the ground of these laws is taken from the *particular constitution of human nature* or from the *accidental circumstances in which such nature is placed.* (Gr 442; 46)

"Rational nature" as distinguished from the *contingencies* of "human nature" exists as an end in itself. Whatever is derived from the "special natural condition of humanity [*der besonderen Naturanlage der Menschheit*]" (Gr 425; 33)—even if it were universal in every respect—could never yield more than a subjective principle (a maxim valid for us). Founded on the knowledge of human nature (founded on mere experience, that is) it could indeed be called a practical rule but never an objective law. In the theoretical realm, where concepts have no significance and principles no use except with respect to objects of experience, speculative reason "may permit [*erlaubt*]" and "even . . . find necessary [*notwendig findet*]" a dependence on human reason; however this dependence is impossible in the practical realm where the concepts of practical reason must apply to all rational beings *without exception.* Indeed, as we are told from the outset—in the opening pages of the Preface to the *Grundlegung*—the concept of morality carries with it an "absolute necessity" or apriority (Gr 389; 2) whose range far exceeds that of any intuition. Moral law is moral, in other words, solely on condition that it apply to all rational beings in general, about whom "no experience is capable of determining anything" (Gr 431; 37).

Thus not only can "rational nature" not be reduced to "human nature" without at the same time stripping morality of its absolute necessity, but, what is more, such an equation bypasses all practical "sources of cognition [*Erkenntnisquellen*]" at their very origin by confusing the concepts of practical reason with the concepts of theoretical reason whose "real possibility" obtains only with respect to objects of human experience (B xxvi). In this way, "rational nature" or "the universal concept of a rational being in general" leaves room for the necessary extension of the rational beyond anything that is "human" strictly speaking. This may of course refer to a host of rational but merely possible beings: God, angels, holy beings, Martians, aliens, extraterrestrials, etc. But it must also, at the same time, refer to an extension, which, though it is not determined by the "human," is *inseparable* from the human[19]–for human beings are rational, even if imperfectly so—and *intrinsic* to the human— for human beings are constitutionally predisposed both to "humanity" and to "personality."[20] In other words, *whether or not* there actually (literally) exist rational beings other than human beings in the world, the existence of "rational nature" can never be reduced to or equated with "human nature." If moral law exists, it exists just it case there exists "something [*etwas*]" that human nature can neither assimilate nor eliminate.

Autonomy is the "ground of the dignity [*Grund der Würde*] of human nature and of every rational nature" (Gr 436; 41). Every rational being has an absolute worth or dignity: it is an end in itself because it is the subject of all ends and thus "at the same time the subject of a possible absolutely good will" (Gr 437; 36). Yet a question is bound to arise. For we are also, at the same time, before a potentially infinite chain of objective and independently existing ends, an abyssal possibility of enumeration. What is, finally, the *relation* between one rational being and the other in this chain? Are all rational beings or ends in themselves identical by definition, that is to say, simply *interchangeable, exchangeable* in their "dignity"? But how can what is absolutely singular be put into a series in which its very singularity becomes replaceable? How can a singularity be both irreplaceable *and* universalizable in its singularity? To be replaceable in its very irreplaceability: is this then the predicament of every singularity?[21] This question seems all the more pertinent when we recall that "dignity" is what distinguishes an object of respect from a thing of barter: "Whatever has a price can be replaced by something as its equivalent; on the other hand, whatever is above all price, and therefore admits of no equivalent, has a dignity" (Gr 434; 40). Are rational beings whose worth is said to be "absolute" invariably and immediately recuperated by a system of exchange and substitution—the economic system of the marketplace according to Kant's example—by the mechanical play (formal logic) of definitions? Or does there exist an *absolute difference* between them?[22] Could there exist, in other words, an absolute difference *between* rational beings? What is, then, the nature of the "relation of rational beings to one another" (Gr 434; 40)? And how does one *pass*—indeed can one pass—from "me" to "every other rational being" without at the same time immediately reducing an absolute worth to a measurable and comparable worth, without, that is, assimilating an intrinsic and irreducible difference to precisely the "same difference"?

Let us return for a moment to Kant's emphatic distinction between "human nature" and "rational nature":

> If then there is to be a supreme practical principle and, as far as the human will is concerned, a categorical imperative, then this supreme practical principle must be such that [*so muß es ein solches sein, das*]— from the conception of what is necessarily an end for everyone, because this end is an *end in itself*—it constitutes [*ausmacht*] an objective principle of the will and can hence serve as a practical law. The ground of such a principle is this: *rational nature exists as an end in itself.* In this way a human being necessarily conceives of his own existence; thus far is it a *subjective* principle of human actions. But in this way also does every other rational being conceive of [*so stellt sich aber auch . . . vor*] its existence on the same rational ground that holds [*gilt*] also for me;[23] hence it is at the same time [*also ist es zugleich*] an *objective* principle, from which, as a supreme practical ground, all laws of the will must be able to be derived. (Gr 428–29; 36)

"But in this way also does every rational being think of its existence . . . hence it is at the same time an *objective* principle": "does" has here, as we have seen, the a priori force of a "must," for without it—without the necessary condition that is met by this "does"— there can be no objective principle. If the moral law is to rest on purely rational grounds, then human existence is beholden for its dignity, its "humanity [*Menschheit*]" (Gr 435; 40), its "proper self [*eigentlichen Selbst*]" (Gr 461; 60) to something to which it can never correspond. "*But* in this way *also*": every other rational being must *also*, like me, by definition, think of its existence as an end in itself, *but* without the fact of this concurrence[24]—the "yes"— of every other rational being without exception there can be no objective principle and thus no moral law strictly speaking. Like the dynamical antinomies in the first *Critique*, the regress is here from grounded (human nature) to ground (rational nature). As a result, however, we are no longer before homogeneous members of the same spatiotemporal series. In other words, because it is constitutive of human nature, rational nature cannot itself be entirely human. "But in this way also does *every rational being* think of its existence": it is not the sum total of existing rational beings that is at issue for Kant but rather rational Being itself (which, as we have seen, is inseparable from but not synonymous with human Being). Rational Being determines the human *because* of its irreducibility to the human. The ground of possibility of all autonomous subjectivity emerges thus from a background of necessary and infinite difference. What this means is that there can be no autonomous subjectivity without infinite difference,[25] no autonomous subjectivity that is not defined in this differential way, and only thus can autonomous subjectivity be something that is not containable or exchangeable. Hence there can be no passage from "me" to "every other rational being," if autonomy is to be, as it must be for Kant, an objective principle of action.

Let us again review the conditions of autonomy in light of human finitude: on the one hand, the will of a finite rational being must be self-grounding, that is, it must not base itself on the contingent existence of anything else, which would make it heteronomous; but, on the other hand and *at the same time*, this will is never purely itself, for, as Kant makes very clear, only a purely rational will, a "divine will" or a "holy will," could contain within itself the possibility of its own fulfillment such that the imperative "ought" (the moral command) would be "out of place [*am unrechten Orte*]" (Gr 414; 24).[26] Indeed only an individual will that could posit itself as its own presupposition and could thereby turn itself into its own ground of determinate laws can be called an autonomous will, "a will that is at once subjective and universal."[27] Subjective *and* universal, subjective *and* self-universalizing, the absolutely subjective will must be able to perform its own universalization: this is what is required of an autonomous will, a will that would emerge *in and as* the connective/hiatus between two incompatible, inseparable demands. In a word, finite autonomy carries within itself not its own fulfillment but its own impossibility, not because it somehow wills its own destruction, but because it is only by *incorporating* the differential power that grounds it that it can become what it must be in order to be itself—*self-grounding*. Let us call this differential power "irrecusable otherness" or "absolute heteronomy,"[28] for it is what makes autonomy autonomy in the first place; it is also what makes self-grounding necessary. Absolute heteronomy lies thus at the heart of all relations (whether it be the subject's relation to itself, to another subject, or to an object); the very distinction between autonomy and heteronomy is founded in *absolute heteronomy*. Just as no moral action can come into being without the principle of autonomy, no principle of autonomy can come into being without a necessary relation to something that is and must remain irreducible to it, a naught of alterity without whose permanence no principle of autonomy, and therefore no moral law could get off the ground.

Kant's theorization of autonomy, furthermore, as I will briefly show, is the literal, textual enactment of this philosophical predicament. Let us return for a moment to the short paragraphs that directly precede the passage concerning subjective and objective principles of action:

> Suppose however that there were something [*Gesetzt aber, es gäbe etwas*] *whose existence* had *in itself* an absolute worth, something which as *an end in itself* could be a ground of determinate laws, such that in it, and in it alone would lie the ground of a possible categorical imperative, that is, of a practical law. (Gr 428; 35)

> Now I say [*Nun sage ich*]: human beings, and in general every rational being *exists* as an end in itself. (Gr 428; 35)

How is it, one cannot help but ask, that at this most fundamental of moments in Kant's argument there appears a dramatic and suspenseful staging—"[s]uppose however there were something"—of the very thing that would alone be capable of grounding moral law? Abruptly, jarringly and no less significantly, this moment of suspended subjunctive possibility is immediately settled in real time by the authoritative declaration of an "I." How is it that Kant assumes as a premise the conclusion that his argument must prove? How can it be, one might ask, that at this point of passage from a history of hypothetical imperatives and principles of heteronomy to "a supreme practical principle and, as far as the human will is concerned, a categorical imperative" (Gr 428; 36), Kant's language is suddenly determined by a sequence of speech acts for which justification is notably absent in the text: a positing (*setzen*) in the first case, and an "expositive" or verdict in the second.[29] What makes this intrusion of the performative all the more remarkable is that it occurs in close proximity to the paragraph on the unwarranted conclusions of subjective positing with which it is entirely incompatible. The unconditioned ground of the supreme practical principle can only be what it is by being given a priori and not "gesetzt," let alone on the basis of a declaration issued by a first person singular. That language should be capable of such performative acts has a long and well documented history, but that Kant's language should have recourse to them here is particularly problematic since in this case what is said (*gesagt*) and supposed (*gesetzt*) holds (*gilt*) and must hold for every rational being at the same time if it is to constitute an objective principle of will and thus a practical law. This is not the voice of reason speaking, a "fearsome [*furchtbare*] voice" (MS 438) that Kant places above and beyond any human voice, a commanding voice, a voice that speaks in the vocative when it speaks. Speaking thus in the first person singular and positing the condition on which its truth depends, "I" does the opposite of what it says and means to say; it instantiates an elaboration that it cannot have. After Kant's repeated and emphatic statements that an "independently existing end" must abstract from all merely subjective ends, we now come upon a passage in which the notion of a "subjective" end—i.e. an end that is here *literally* posited by subject who says "I"—takes an ironic and surprising turn, to say the least. We are left, in other words, with a linguistic fact that, wherever it comes from, no longer comes from within an autonomous legislation of linguistic reason.

Absolute heteronomy appears, as we have seen, in/as the very genesis of autonomy, as the limiting condition of the possibility of autonomy. The irreducibility of absolute heteronomy must be *passed over* by Kant in the name of the self-sameness, the unity of reason itself—"for in the final analysis there can only be one and the same reason" (Gr 391; 4). The existence of an absolute and unassimilable other to which autonomy owes its possibility is passed over, but it is at the same time *passed on* to us quite literally as an unassimilable philosophical predicament (here, for example, as a force of literality that remains perfectly legible in Kant's text). Absolute heteronomy must remain absolute, it must remain irreducible to autonomy, transmissible, that is, *only* in its impassability, which is to say passable as a legacy in which absolute alterity is played out not in theory but in the very practice of reading. Just as Kant imparts to us the only principle of autonomy—"das alleinige Prinzip der Moral" (Gr 440; 44)—that is, the source of all non-spurious principles of morality, so he leaves us,[30] at the same time, with a legacy of absolute heteronomy to which, I will claim, we are now summoned to respond.[31]

The Legacy of Kant

Disappointed and dismayed by the non-reception of his major work, Kant will defend the *Critique of Pure Reason* in the Preface to its second edition (1787) precisely in terms of its "legacy." "What sort of a treasure [*Schatz*] is this," Kant will ask, "that we propose to bequeath to posterity [*der Nachkommenschaft . . . hinterlassen*]?" (B xxiv). What is to have been gained by a critique of pure reason? What is to have been acquired by a metaphysics purified through criticism? Kant will then instruct his reader that although it may not be terribly difficult to "leave to posterity the legacy [*der Nachkommenschaft ein Vermächtnis zu hinterlassen*] of a systematic metaphysics, constructed in conformity with a critique of pure reason," still such a bequest is a "gift [*Geschenk*] deserving of no small respect" (B xxx). It is true, Kant tells us, that insofar as the *Critique* warns the reader that speculative reason must never venture beyond the boundaries of experience, its teaching seems to be wholly negative. But this teaching immediately acquires a positive value, for it simultaneously removes an obstacle that threatens to wipe out even the possibility of a "moral [use]" (B xxv) of reason. The legacy of the first *Critique* is thus a moral legacy; it is a criticism of pure reason and already the possibility of an extension of pure reason. It marks a threshold: a threshold that is described most famously by Kant as the procurement of a space—a space that emerges from the work of the *Critique* itself—"speculative reason has thus at least made room for such an extension, even if it had to leave it empty [*die speculative hat . . . zu solcher Erweiterung immer doch wenigstens Platz vershafft, wenn sie ihn gleich leer lassen mußte*]" (B xxi). This space of possibility, which must be left empty or blank by speculative reason, should be filled, however—for "nature itself . . . abhors a vacuum [*das Leere*]," as Kant tells us in *The Metaphysics of Morals* (MS 267; 87). Indeed we are called upon, requested, invited, summoned, challenged, "aufgefordert" (B xxii) to do just this by reason itself.

The space left empty by the *Critique of Pure Reason* is peculiar, however, for it is its very emptiness that gives rise to the possibility of practical reason. Were it not for this space, freedom and with it morality would have to give way to the mechanism of nature. Only by way of this emptiness, in other words, does the *Critique of Pure Reason* constitute a legacy and thus the future of moral possibility. This should not surprise us, however, for as Kant explains in *The Metaphysics of Morals*, emptiness literally constitutes the space of passage required of all legacies. In any practical use of reason where the relation involves a contract or continuity between rational beings, one encounters this empty space. Kant will even give it a Latin name: it is a "res vacua" without which a legacy is inconceivable according to Right.

However, because we are still in the epistemological context of the *Critique of Pure Reason,* a question arises: what is a legacy or a bequest, a last will and testament, what is a "Vermächtnis"—the "Vermächtnis" of a systematic metaphysics, for example—that is not *already* a practical use of reason? How, in other words, is practical reason to precede its own possibility? How does practical reason become heir to itself? Are we to understand Kant's repeated bequest as just another figure of speech?

I will argue on the contrary that an excessive and most radical possibility suggests itself here. For if this space is indeed the space of *legacy,* as Kant insists it is, then two very different stories result from Kant's bequest. On the one hand, we have a figurative, historical narrative that describes the resolution of an epistemological tension in the positing of the possibility of freedom from a practical perspective; and on the other hand but at the same time, we have the allegory of the (im)possibility of this first story. Indeed, according to this second reading, the legacy of a systematic metaphysics would usher in its own possibility.

The problem of "legacy" remains thus, one might say, both "the *keystone*" (Schlußstein) and the "stumbling stone" (*Stein des Anstoßes*) of the whole system of pure reason. In an effort to address this paradoxical duality—and it must be addressed since the very possibility of practical reason is bound up with it—let us begin by turning to Kant's own writing on the topic in *The Metaphysics of Morals.*

INHERITING A LEGACY

As Kant makes clear to an "astute critic" in an appendix to the "Doctrine of Right" in his "Explanatory Remarks on *The Metaphysical First Principles of the Doctrine of Right*" (MS 356; 163),[32] an "inheritance [*Beerbung*]" should not to be confused with an unqualified gain nor even, for that matter, with something whose desirability can be assumed. Indeed the legacy which I inherit might be something I would prefer to decline—"because its acceptance [*Annahme*] might involve me in unpleasantness with others"

(MS 366; 171). What I acquire unavoidably by inheritance is thus not a thing (desirable or undesirable) but only the exclusive right to accept or refuse this thing. Inheritance confers on me a right, and this right is "exclusive [*ausschließlich*]": on the one hand, as Kant says, such exclusivity must be conceived of as "an enriching circumstance [*Vermögensumstand*]" because "the authorization to accept [*die Befugnis zu akzeptieren*]" belongs to me alone (MS 366; 171). On the other hand, however, this exclusivity singles me out for an acquisition I cannot refuse, for the right to choose whether I will or will not have the legacy in question is "mine" regardless of my choice; my desire to be possessed of such a choice, in other words, has no bearing on the possibility of my chosenness. The exclusive authorization to accept or refuse a legacy is not something I choose; rather it is my election to a necessity of choice.

An act of inheritance, if it occurs, is thus an extraordinary act: not only because it involves taking a legacy upon oneself and into the intimacy of one's possession but because it elicits from the will a response to a chosenness that is not of its own making. Although I cannot refuse to have this choice (were such the case, "I would be choosing not to choose, which is a contradiction" [MS 366; 171–72]), it is equally true that by a unilateral will alone nothing at all can pass to another person. As Kant explains in a paragraph entitled "Inheritance," for a legacy to be passed on to another person there is still required, in addition to the promise of the testator: an "acceptance (*acceptatio*) by the other party and a simultaneous will [*ein gleichzeitiger Wille*] (*voluntas simultanea*)" (MS 294; 110). Like all external acquisition by contract, acquisition by inheritance involves *two* acts of will. An act of acceptance is required, which is to say, an act whereby the chosen heir receives the "legacy [*Verlassenschaft*]" as her own and brings it back within a fixed and stable dominion—to a resting place, as it were. This act of will is required because until possessorship has been properly reclaimed, the legacy remains suspended; "it hovers," "[sie] schwebt," "between acceptance and rejection [*zwischen der Annahme und der Verwerfung*]" (MS 294; 111).

Transfer [*Die Translation*] is therefore an act in which an object belongs, for a moment, to both [parties] together, just as when a stone that has been thrown reaches the apex of its parabolic path it can be regarded as, for just a moment, simultaneously rising and falling, and so passing from its rising motion to its falling. (MS 274; 93)[33]

[B]oth acts, promise and acceptance, are represented not as following one upon another but ... as proceeding from a single *common* will (this is expressed by the word *simultaneously* [*welches durch das Wort* zugleich *ausgedruckt wird*]) and the object (*promissum*) is represented, by omitting empirical conditions, as acquired in accordance with a principle of pure practical reason. (MS 273; 92)

Such a transfer, Kant insists, can never be empirical because an empirical transfer—dependent upon conditions of space and time (and therefore unable to determine the rightfulness of a relation according to unchanging principles)—must always assume two successive acts following each other in time, "namely the act by which one person first leaves his possessions [*seinen Besitz verläßt*] and the other then comes into them [*darin eintritt*]" (MS 293; 110). Were the transfer in question empirical, the second party would only ever acquire something that had ceased to belong to anyone and hence would acquire it originally, through an act of unilateral will (*occupatio*), and this would contradict the very notion of inheritance.

In the time without time of my acceptance (or refusal), thus, the bequest becomes a possession in abeyance: "the bequest [*Erbschaft*] has not become altogether possessorless [*herrenlos*] (*res nullius*) in the meantime ["while it hovers between acceptance and rejection"] but only vacant [*erledigt*] (*res vacua*)" (MS 294; 110). It is not a thing that belongs to no one but a thing suspended: not yet abandoned by the one, not again reclaimed by the other. The passing on or carrying over of a legacy depends on a "moment" or "space" of simultaneity that lies neither in time nor in space (an act of transfer is a purely intellectual relation) but whose condition grounds the possibility of inheritance. The price of passage is heavy, moreover, since it now rests entirely on this concept of an empty space, a "res vacua."

It is now the concept of "res vacua" that makes the line between the "not yet" and "no longer" (MS 272; 92) of all empirical transfers passable (and impassable—except by recourse to this "res vacua").[34]

One must begin, therefore, by distinguishing between a "res vacua" and a "res nullius." Can a serious distinction be drawn between them, as Kant claims? The answer to the above question might be "yes and no."[35] And yet, as we will see, if the distinction between that which allows for continuous possession ("res vacua") and that which does not ("res nullius") can no longer be contained within a doctrine of Right, then the moment or space of legacy must also carry with it something that is not "possessed" in the usual sense.

"[T]he bequest has not become altogether possessorless (*res nullius*) ... but only vacant (*res vacua*)" (MS 294; 110). A "res vacua," says Kant, is not a "res nullius." But what is a "res nullius"? Kant first introduces the concept in the first chapter of the "Doctrine of Right" where it plays an essential role in establishing the a priori grounds of a system of Right. Indeed, in a system of Right, no possible "object of choice [*Gegenstand meiner Willkür*]" can be called a "res nullius." Any object of choice must "rightfully [*rechtlich*]" be within my power to use, for if its use were "wrong [*unrecht*],"

> then freedom would be depriving itself of the use of its choice [*ihrer Willkür*] with regard to an object of choice, by putting *usable* objects beyond any possibility of being used; in other words, it would *annihilate* [vernichtete] them in a practical respect and make them into *res nullius*, even though in the use of things [*im Gebrauch der Sachen*] choice was formally consistent with everyone's outer freedom in accordance with universal laws. (MS 246; 69)

Turning an "object of choice" into a "res nullius" would be thus to contradict the universal law of freedom. It must therefore be an a priori presupposition of practical reason to regard any object of choice as a possible possession (granted it has not yet been claimed by another); in other words, the "postulate of practical reason with regard to rights" is a principle that gives us the "authorization [*Befugnis*]" (MS 247; 69) to rightfully claim any object of our choice as our own. Such a claim, Kant argues, would be inconceivable (and thus impossible from a practical point of view) were objects of choice to be considered "res nullius." Because the condition of possibility of "res nullius" is the condition of impossibility of intelligible possession—because, that is, "res nullius" is the contradictory of an object of choice—the possibility of possession (*possessio noumenon*) rests on an "original community of land in general [*die ursprüngliche Gemeinschaft des Bodens überhaupt*]" (MS 262; 84), for only this common possession contains the a priori principle according to which humans can acquire a place on earth "in conformity with principles of Right [*Rechtsgesetzen*]" (MS 262; 84). Thus "the *rational title* [Vernunfttitel]" (MS 264; 85) of acquisition in general requires—in addition to the possibility of intelligible possession—both the "postulate of practical reason with regard to rights" according to which any object of my choice (that does not already belong to another) can be mine and the "*lawgiving* [Gesetzgebung]" of a will that is "united a priori [a priori vereinigt]" (MS 267; 87). The conditions of possibility of acquisition in general—and, consequently, the conditions of possibility of acquisition by contract, "last will or testament [*Vermächtnis*]" (MS 293; 110)—must begin with the formal exclusion of all "res nullius."

An object of choice can never be a "res nullius." Kant gives several examples of this. The neutral land between two peoples "is not something *belonging to no one* [herrenlos] (*res nullius*)" since it really belongs to "both in common [*beiden gemeinschaftlich*]" and is "being *used* by both [*von beiden . . . gebraucht wird*]" (MS 265; 86) in order to keep the other at a safe distance. Neither can "the thing [*die Sache*]" that a shorefront owner finds washed up on her land "be treated as a *res nullius*" (MS 270; 90). Perhaps only the high seas, which are free (*mare liberum*), could ever fulfill such a condition in reality, and even here, as Kant acknowledges, freedom from possession would only begin on the far side of a cannon's reach from shore (MS 269; 89–90).

Following Kant's worldly examples, however, before the section "On Property Right" can be brought to a close, a point in need of further (and immediate) elucidation seems suddenly to arise. This point is one that Kant himself judges to be out of place: "This is not ... the proper place to discuss this point [*dieser Punkt hat hier nicht seinen eigentlichen Platz*]"; indeed "[i]t is mentioned only incidentally [*beiläufig*]" as a way of explaining "what was discussed a little earlier" (MS 270; 90), namely the conditions regarding possessorship of an external object of choice. In a distinction that will prove very familiar to readers of the *Grundlegung*, Kant draws attention here, in this place out of place, to the incommensurability between, on the one hand, an external thing that belongs to someone as "his *property* [Eigentum] (*dominium*)" and that can be disposed of as he pleases, and, on the other hand, a person, who may well be his own master (*sui iuris*) but who can never be the owner of himself (*sui dominus*) such that he may dispose of himself as he pleases.[36] A person is never free to do with himself as he pleases, for he is always "answerable for the humanity in his own person [*weil er der Menschheit in seiner eigenen Person verantwortlich ist*]" (MS 270; 90). By virtue of a morally practical reason, i.e. as the subject of a possible absolutely good will, a person "possesses [*besitzt*] an inalienable dignity [*eine unverlierbare Würde*] (*dignitas interna*)" (MS 436; 231), which is to say, "an absolute inner worth [*einen absoluten innern Wert*]" (MS 435; 230). Once again there arises—in perhaps typically untimely fashion[37]—an imperative to distinguish between an external object or corporeal thing "to which one has no obligation" (MS 270; 90) and a person who must always be regarded and treated as an "object of respect [*Objekt der Achtung*]" (MS 435; 230). Perhaps it is the history of "res" itself that calls forth Kant's needed clarification: used to designate a state of affairs in the broadest sense (*die Sache*) or a thing (*Ding*), "res" is also used by Descartes to describe the I—the ego is a *res cogitans*—such that subject as well as object can be a "res." This time, however, the distinction between an object of choice and an object of respect must be drawn in terms of *possession*. In the case of an external object of choice, where any object that does not already belong to another can be brought under my control and thereby into my possession—the object in question is on the receiving end of a transitive verb. In the case of an object of respect, on the other hand, where possession is also in question, it is the "object" that "possesses [*besitzt*]." It "possesses [*besitzt*]" an inalienable dignity (in the sense of *being* "im Besitze von"—"Every human being *possessed of* reason," as Coleridge says), and it is the particularity of this possession, this being possessed of dignity, that deflects and defies any would-be transitive possession by another including oneself, for self-possession is, in this sense, as we have seen, a moral outrage. This difference of possession, a difference in the possession of an object, comes suddenly as an interruption in Kant's account of "res nullius." And it is the unexpected place of this irruption that suddenly puts us before a possibility of possession that is at the same time not a possession but rather a dis-possession, an Ent-setzung. And it is this possibility of (dis)possession, a possibility that is "entsetzlich,"[38] that suggests to us a "res nullius" of an entirely different order. For in this context, one might conclude that humanity is itself the "res nullius" par excellence.

The attempt to distinguish between a "res vacua" and a "res nullius"—between the "res" that allows for possession and the "res" that does not—thus carries us over (back) into the moral realm; it immediately gives rise to another question, indeed a question that is far more fundamental and on which this distinction itself depends: Would a legacy convey something other than what a testator possesses as a thing? Could one bequeath something that one did not "possess"? One might say that the intrusion of the moral in the very definition of "possession" is something that is not and cannot be possessed. One might go so far as to say that *dispossession* is the legacy that founds the human. What would be the epistemological impact of such a legacy?

POSSESSION

> The body is mine because it is part of my I and is moved through my free will [*Willkür*]. The whole animate or inanimate world which has not its own free will is mine insofar as I can compel it and move it according to my free will. The sun is not mine.[39]

In what is perhaps the most central and decentering of sections in *The Metaphysics of Morals*, §13 of the "Doctrine of Virtue," Kant describes the defining feature of humanity as its singular double-ness, its "dual personality [*zwiefache Persönlichkeit*]." Indeed, as he explains, "the human being who accuses and judges himself in conscience must conceive of himself" as a "doubled self [*doppelte Selbst*]" (MS 439; 234). According to Kant's metaphor, conscience is the consciousness of being possessed of an internal "tribunal [*Gerichtshof*]" (MS 438; 233):

> Every human being has a conscience . . . and this power [*Gewalt*] watch-ing over the law in him is not something that he himself (voluntarily) *makes*, but something incorporated [*einverleibt*] into his very being. It follows him like his shadow when he thinks to flee it. He can in-deed numb himself to it through pleasures and distractions, or by falling asleep, but he cannot avoid awakening [*erwachen*] . . . and when he does, he immediately perceives its fearsome [*furchtbare*] voice. He can . . . bring himself to *heed* it no longer, but he cannot avoid [*ver-meiden*] *hearing* it . . . . Thus, for all duties, the conscience of a human being will have to conceive of something *other* (than human beings as such), that is, other than himself as judge of his actions, if conscience is not to be in contradiction with itself. (MS 438; 233–34)

No finite rational being can avoid being possessed of a conscience. No finite rational being can avoid having or perceiving this non-human, non-sensible, non-pathological voice: a "fearsome voice," a voice that is not a human voice but the voice of an *other*, something "other"—than what is called "human."[40] A human being is defined in its humanity by its very inability to avoid hearing this voice, a voice that is as "unavoidable [*unvermeidlich*]" as it is "involuntary [*unwillkürlich*]" (MS 401; 202). One does not choose this voice; rather one is chosen by it. It is a given of humanity. Since it is by nature an "inexorable fact [*unausbleibliche Tatsache*]" (MS 400; 201), it cannot be a duty to have a conscience. Rather it lies at the base of morality as a "*subjective* condition" of our susceptibility, of our "receptiveness [*Empfänglichkeit*]" (MS 399; 201) to the very concept of duty. In this way, conscience is a "natural predisposition of the mind (*praedisposito*) for being affected by concepts of duty" (MS 399; 200–01). Indeed no human being can be completely lacking in such susceptibility, for such a human being according to Kant, a being with no basic moral feeling whatsoever, would be "morally dead [*sittlich tot*]" (MS 400; 201). Or worse yet:

> [I]f (to speak in *medical* terms) the moral vital force could no longer excite this [moral] feeling, then humanity would *dissolve* [auflösen] (by *chemical laws*, as it were) into mere animality and be *mixed irretrievably* [unwiederbringlich vermischt] with the mass of other natural beings. (MS 400; 201, my emphasis)

Without even the most basic of necessary predispositions, one is no longer speaking of the human but of an accident of nature, as Hegel might say.

The consciousness we have of our conscience is not, however, of empirical origin, for it only follows from the consciousness of the moral law—which is to say, as the effect that this law has on the human mind. Conscience is not consciousness of a self but rather consciousness of the differential relation that splits the self from it-self and guarantees this differential existence in the shadow existence of a power, a power that is first and foremost a "something" and an "it":

> [A]nd this power [*Gewalt*] watching over the law in him is not something [*etwas, was*] that he himself (voluntarily) *makes*, but something [*es*] incorporated [*einverleibt*] into his very being. It [*Es*] follows him like his shadow when he thinks to flee it.

This power is not something one makes (one's choice or will is not involved whether we read "willkürlich" as "voluntary" or as "arbitrary"); it is not something made and not something in which any consciousness or self-consciousness of a subject as maker could ever be active.[41] Rather—and this is an extraordinarily momentous occurrence—something that is "incorporated [*einverleibt*]" into a human being. Incorporation preserves intact the otherness, the "it-ness" of this power: it is in me, integral to my being as human and it always impinges on me from within, but it is not "mine," it is not me nor is it assimilable to me, to my I. What is incorporated is "a power [*Gewalt*]" whose voice dominates and causes its host to stand in fear, "trembling [*zitternd*]" before its verdict (MS 439; 234). "It follows him like his shadow"—like his shadow, this power is the sign of an encounter between a *homo phaenomenon* and the sun (whose standpoint only reason can take); it is a material haunting. There is no escaping this shadow since it is incorporated into one's fleshly being. Even the most concerted effort to stupefy and deaden one's natural being to the voice of conscience is doomed from the start, since incorporation is the very condition and continuation of this effort. And even if one succeeds for a time, there always and inevitably comes an "awakening" and with it the return of the "fearsome voice."

There is nothing exalted or divine about this voice, however— it is not "a veiled Isis" (Ton 405; 71). It is not "an other, whose essence is unknown to us" (Ton 405; 71) but the most powerful expression of practical law stemming from reason itself. This voice that is perceived from reason is what *makes* human beings rational beings; it is that which refuses any totalization of either what is called "human nature" or what is called "rational nature." By giving voice to the differential relation that is humanity, *conscience is thus heir* to the irreducibly dual conditions of moral possibility that we identified in the first section of this chapter. A human being awakens to conscience/consciousness and immediately perceives its "fearsome" voice. This voice is "fearsome" not because of its strangeness (it is all too familiar to us) but because of its relentless pursuit of a hearing: it is that which refuses to be passed over in silence. It defies all assimilation by the body. It is not a thing that can be possessed; rather it is an other that possesses me, an other *by which and of which* I am possessed. It comes to me, to me exclusively (which is to say, me exclusively every time, an infinite number of times) from the completely other in me and disturbs the silence— indeed, as Kant says, "the conscience of a human being will have to conceive of something *other* (than human beings as such)... if conscience is not to be in contradiction with itself" (MS 438; 234).

LAST WILL AND TESTAMENT

If conscience is not to be in contradiction with itself, what is "other" than the human as such must be incorporated into the human and yet remain "other." The "dual personality" of human beings is for Kant this impossibility made possible:

> This requires further comment, if reason is not to fall into contradiction with itself. *I,* the prosecutor [*Ich, der Kläger*] and yet the accused as well, *am* the same being [*bin eben derselbe Mensch*] (*numero idem*) but, *as subject* of the moral lawgiving [*als* Subjekt *der moralischen Gesetzgebung*] which proceeds from the concept of freedom and in which a human being is subordinated to a law that he gives himself (*homo noumenon*), *he is* [ist er] to be regarded as other [*als ein anderer*] than the sensible being endowed with reason (*specie diversus*), though only in a practical respect. (MS 439n; 234n)

But a question inevitably arises, for this further "comment" or "clarification [*Erläuterung*]," as Kant calls it, only obscures the problem. Indeed, Kant's explanation rests on an agrammatical construction. It moves from an "I"—"I, the prosecutor"—to a phrase that stands in *suspended apposition*—"as subject of the moral lawgiving"—to a "he"—"he is to be regarded as other than the sensible being endowed with reason." Suspended, oscillating, *torn* between the "I" and the "he" is none other than "the subject of the moral lawgiving," i.e. the very term that was to bind them. How are we to read this non-passage from "I" to "he" (neatly elided in the English translation)? How can we be so sure of a return to sameness when the impossibility made possible seems to overflow its boundaries and contradict its assertions? Is "I" "Subjekt" or is "he"? It seems, at the very least, "difficult" to keep this impossibility in check. And yet autonomy itself hinges on the possibility of "he" being contained within the "I" and thus not "he" at all. Kant has literally turned the "I" into another person here. Could this slip be intentional, a rigorous display of the duality in question? Are we then to read this slip figuratively, no longer as a slip, that is, but as an intention? Or are we to read it literally—true to the letter of Kant's text—as the unintentional (and for a theory of autonomy, certainly undesirable) *actual* emergence of something "other" in the form of another person? However we read it, there is something "fearsome" about this occurrence. For it has now given voice to what cannot be the case and yet, conversely, what must be the case if the internal judge is to remain the "other" in me. The fearsome voice of conscience is precisely this linguistic predicament: the "he," the "it" that dispossess the "I" of itself. The possibility of such a dual personality, Kant tells us, can be considered "only in a practical respect," for there can be no "theory" about the causal relation of the intelligible to the sensible (MS 439; 234). And yet, for this splitting to be conceivable from a practical standpoint, "I" must unify self and other (one is reminded here of Schelling's notion of "identity," which is still profoundly Kantian). Only thus does the impossible become possible in a practical respect. But "I" (*numero idem*), as we have seen, precisely fails both to subsume and to erase the trace of the completely "other," a trace that remains exceedingly legible. "[A]s subject of the moral lawgiving ... *he* is ... to be regarded as other than the sensible being endowed with reason."

CODA

> It's exactly what we can't reinsert into interiority, into the homogeneity of some protected place.[42]

One must conclude that such an emergence—the fact of conscience in the actual dispossession of an "I"—is not without epistemological impact. I can only suggest here that such a dispossession (whether it is figurative or literal, a success or a failure, a triumph or a fall) in the fearsome voice of a third person that appears suddenly in Kant's text points to another epistemology, a "second" epistemology—one in which absolute heteronomy is never simply passed over but always also passed on. Indeed I would suggest that the voice of conscience is itself heir to absolute heteronomy, and that humanity—"insofar as it is capable of morality" (Gr 435; 40–41)—is a memorial to this inheritance. Although it is "something *other* (than human beings in general)," the otherness of conscience cannot be opposed to human beings: on the contrary, as we seen, it is neither reducible to nor separable from what is called "the human." But it is no longer the self's "other," a transcendental "other" that can be fully determined by or contained within an "I," as Kant's texts have demonstrated. Absolute heteronomy is not an impossibility made possible. Rather it is a possibility that remains "other" qua possibility, a possibility that is not of this world and yet in this world, *a possibility beyond possibility* that always leaves a trace. With the emergence of this decentering possibility, a possibility that turns the self's other into an other "other" and refuses any known measure of the human, one encounters the true legacy of Kant, a legacy, which—as the legacy of legacy—always carries with it a terrible risk, for it is the legacy of the future.

§ 2 Freud

When Morality Makes Us Sick: Disavowal, Ego Splitting, and the Tragedy of Obsessional Neurosis

Im Traum und in der Neurose pocht dieses Ausgeschlossene
um Einlaß an den ... Pforten.

> — (Sigmund Freud, *Massenpsychologie und Ich-Analyse*)

Si nous revenons toujours à Freud, c'est parce qu'il est parti
d'une intuition initiale, centrale, qui est d'ordre éthique.

> — (Jacques Lacan, *L'éthique de la psychanalyse*)[1]

Why is it that thinkers in the field of ethics always return to the problem of pleasure and to the relation of pleasure to the final good? To what should we attribute the internal demand that constrains not only Kant but also moral philosophers in general to reduce the antinomies associated with these themes? Might it not be possible for human beings to think ethics "beyond the pleasure principle"? As these questions seek to make explicit, psychoanalysis has its place—an important place—in any discussion of ethics. It is certainly interesting to note the regularity with which the problem of pleasure arises in these discussions. However, it is not Freud's theory of the ego's repression *(Verdrängung)* of the instinctual demands of the pleasure principle that provides psychoanalysis with its greatest insight into the question of morality. Rather it is the power of Freud's analysis of the ego's ability to disavow an external reality in the particular case of obsessional neurosis. Indeed, as I will argue in this chapter, Freud's late discovery of the psychical mechanism he calls "disavowal [*Verleugnung*]" offers us something unmatched in significance for the study of ethics: the example and workings of a "moral illness."

What might disavowal tell us about reality? What is it exactly that obsessional neurosis defends against? In this chapter, I will show how Freud's analysis of "disavowal," which begins as a story of fetishism and of the reality of sexual difference, gives way to another story and another reality whose implications are distinctly moral.

Defense: An Introduction

When the term "defense [*Abwehr*]" makes its first appearance in psychoanalytic literature, it does so in the very specific context of Freud's 1894 study "The Neuro-Psychoses of Defense." In this early work, the term "defense" is used to describe the ego's struggle against what Freud calls "an instance of incompatibility [*ein Fall von Unverträglichkeit*]" (SE 3: 47). Whether this instance occurs as "an experience, a representation, or a sensation" (SE 3: 47), the incompatibility proves so distressing to the ego that the ego can only protect itself by repudiating what has occurred. Although Freud later abandons the term and replaces it with that of "repression," the old concept of "defense" re-emerges more than thirty years later in "Inhibitions, Symptoms and Anxiety" where Freud uses it to restrict the concept of "repression." "Defense" now refers to all defensive processes including that of "repression," which it includes as "a special case [*Specialfall*]" (SE 20: 164): "It is useful [*zweckmässig*] here to distinguish the more general notion [*Tendenz*] of 'defense [*Abwehr*]' from 'repression [*Verdrängung*],' which is only one of the mechanisms that defense makes use of" (SE 20: 114). There are important, historical reasons for this shift, and, as Freud remarks, for keeping the once-exchangeable concepts distinct:

> The revival of the concept of defense and the restriction of the concept of repression takes into account a fact which has long since been known but which has gained in significance owing to some new discoveries. Our first observations of repression and symptom formation were

made in connection with hysteria. We saw that the perceptual content of exciting experiences and the representational content of pathogenic structures of thought were forgotten and barred [*ausgeschlossen*] from being reproduced in memory, and we therefore concluded that the keeping away [*Abhaltung*] from consciousness was a main characteristic of hysterical repression. Later on, when we came to study the obsessional neuroses, we found that in that illness pathogenic occurrences are not forgotten. They remain conscious but they are "isolated" in some way that we cannot as yet grasp.... We have seen, too ... a procedure, that may be called magical, of "making unhappened [*Ungeschehenmachen*]"—a procedure about whose defensive purpose there can be no doubt, but which has no longer any resemblance to the process of "repression." (SE 20: 163–64)

Thus it is the study of obsessional neurosis that provides Freud with the grounds for reviving the old concept of defense. Freud also makes two additional points regarding the significance of "naming [*Namengebung*]" here. From a *clinical* standpoint, he says, it is important to maintain the difference between "defense" and "repression" because "further investigations may show that there is an intimate connection between special forms of defense and particular illnesses, as for instance, between repression and hysteria" (SE 20: 164). Moreover, Freud continues, there are *theoretical* reasons for keeping the terms distinct. In addition to the possibility of discovering connections between specific illnesses and specific defensive processes, one must keep open the possibility of another kind of connection, a connection of an entirely different order:

We may also look forward to the possibility of another significant connection [*einer anderen bedeutsamen Abhängigkeit*]. It may well be that before its sharp cleavage [*Sonderung*] into an ego and an id, and before the formation of a superego, the mental apparatus makes use of different methods of defense from those which it employs after it has reached these stages of organization. (SE 20: 164)

What Freud is asking us to consider here is the possibility of a defense more primary than repression, a mode of defense that would precede repression and date back to the pre-history of the ego's differentiating processes. When we recall that the theory of repression is among the fundamental postulates and hypotheses of psychoanalysis—when we read that "[t]he theory of repression is the cornerstone on which the whole structure of psychoanalysis rests" (SE 14: 16)—we must conclude that it is not only the future of the ego but the future of psychoanalysis itself that is bound up with such a possibility.

Defending Against the Incompatible

Freud's early use of term "defense" describes a form of reaction so extreme that the ego finds itself in an impossible position:

> For these patients whom I analyzed had enjoyed good mental health up to the moment at which *an instance of incompatibility* [ein Fall von Unverträglichkeit] *occurred in their representational life*—that is to say, until an experience, a representation, or a sensation came upon the ego, which awakened [*erwekte*] such a distressing affect that the person decided to forget it [*beschloß, daran zu vergessen*] because he had no confidence in his power [*Kraft*] to resolve the contradiction between that incompatible representation and his ego by means of thought-activity. (SE 3: 47)

In order to survive, the ego must forget the distress it defends against. Impossible, says Freud, and not only can the ego *not* forget, but it *has not* forgotten: in all of the cases to which Freud refers, the necessary forgetting "did not succeed" but led rather to "various pathological reactions which produced either hysteria or an obsession or a hallucinatory psychosis" (SE 3: 48). In these cases, or in these psychopathologies, not only has the ego been unable to keep the incompatible representation from arriving—unable, as Freud says, "of treating the incompatible representation as '*non arrivée*'" (SE 3: 48)—but the ego has registered the distress it defends against in the form of a symptom (what Hans Loewald calls "enactive remembering," or what Nietzsche calls "active forgetting"). In hysteria, in obsessional neurosis, and in hallucinatory psychosis, both the memory trace and the affect of the representation remain; they are "there once and for all and cannot be eradicated" (SE 3: 48). The ego has not forgotten its distress; it has not fended off the occurrence of incompatibility. And yet it has survived. Freud explains this paradoxical outcome by showing that the defensive process in these cases is always "bound up with a splitting of consciousness [*mit Bewußtseinsspaltung verbunden ist*]" (SE 3: 48). If consciousness is split, it becomes not only possible but also necessary to say, simultaneously, that the ego *has* and *has not* forgotten its distress. In these cases, one might say that the forgetting by the ego is *remembered* in the form of a splitting of consciousness.

Freud will often speak of these defensive methods as being "successful" insofar as the ego accomplishes the immediate task at hand, which is to drive the pathogenic representation out of association. Once an interruption of the connection in thought has been accomplished, once a representation has been removed from all associative networks of psychic life (removing it, thus, from the possibility of being worked through by normal processes of defense), the ego has indeed succeeded in its task. In cases of hysteria and obsessional neurosis, the ego's defense against the incompatible representation is accomplished by separating the representation from its affect. Although neither representation nor affect[2] can be eradicated, they can be split off from one another. In both hysteria and obsessional neurosis, the ego finds an approximate solution to its task by turning a powerful representation into a weak one. By "robbing [*entreißen*]" the representation of its affect, by "wrenching" its affect from it, the ego is left with a weak and unthreatening representation (SE 3: 48–49). However, the sum of excitation that has been detached from the representation must still be mobilized. In the case of hysteria, "the oldest, the best-known and the most striking" of the psycho-neuroses (SE 2: 258), the ego's solution involves transforming the sum of excitation into a somatic innervation. The incompatible representation is repressed—it is kept out of consciousness—and it is rendered innocuous by converting its affect into something somatic (thus, the hysterical process is called a "conversion"). If, however, one has a neurotic disposition but one lacks "the aptitude for conversion [*die Eignung zur Konversion*]," all is not lost, for obsessional neurosis offers yet another solution. Although the affect will remain in consciousness, it will attach itself to representations that are not in themselves incompatible with the ego. And it is this "false connection" that turns these substitute representations into "obsessional representations" (SE 3: 52). In an obsessional neurosis, affect is "dislodged [*disloziert*]" or "transposed [*transponiert*]" (SE 3: 54) from its original representation, and it is precisely "this *mésalliance* between the emotional state and the associated idea that accounts for the *absurdity* so characteristic of obsessions," Freud writes in 1895 (SE 3: 75, my emphasis). Although both hysteria and obsessional neurosis seem equally (partially) successful, neither transposition nor conversion of affect can compare to what Freud proposes as solution number three.

For there is yet a third method for dealing with the incompatible representation, one in which the representation is banished from consciousness altogether. "There is . . . a much more energetic and successful kind of defense [*eine weit energische und erfolgreichere Art der Abwehr*]," Freud proclaims (SE 3: 58). Indeed, in this most successful of defenses, the *nec plus ultra* of defensive methods, the ego refuses the incompatible representation, which it throws out (*verwirft*) along with its affect. The subject behaves as if the representation had never occurred to the ego. "*But from the moment at which this has been successfully done the subject is in a psychosis*" (SE 3: 58).

Hence one is justified in saying, as Freud will, that the ego "has fended off [*abgewehrt hat*]" the incompatible representation through "a flight into psychosis" (SE 3: 59). Once "the defense has been happily successful [*nach glücklich gelungener Abwehr*]," the person will be in a state of hallucinatory confusion (SE 3: 60). I would like to suggest here that, in the ego's paroxysm of success, it becomes necessary to distinguish between a psychological success, in which even the psychotic is able to survive a traumatic incompatibility, and what might better be called an actual "failure," in which an occurrence of incompatibility not only cannot be reversed—"both the memory trace and the affect which is attached to the representation are there once and for all and cannot be eradicated [*sind einmal da und nicht mehr auszutilgen*]" (SE 3: 48)—but whose very force is registered by the tragic irony of psychological success.

On the one hand, thus, as Freud says, the ego succeeds in its task, which is to drive the incompatible representation out of association (a partial success in the case of hysteria and obsessional neurosis, a more complete success in the case of psychosis); on the other hand, however, Freud's ironic tone says just the opposite, for this flight into illness is a miserable failure. It is a failure in terms of the suffering of the psyche (in hysteria, obsessional neurosis, or psychosis), but it is also a failure insofar as the illness remains a constant and living reminder of what has not and cannot be forgotten. The ego must solve an insoluble dilemma: "the task that the ego, in its defensive attitude, sets itself of treating the incompatible representation as '*non arrivée*' is for the ego simply insoluble [*direkt unlösbar*]" (SE 3: 48). The ego's charge, as we have seen, is to treat as "non arrivée" an instance of incompatibility whose very arrival makes such treatment necessary. It must make non-arrive what has already arrived. What must not arrive has already arrived. Thus, the "*instance of incompatibility*"[3] that is at the heart of the defensive process from its very beginning suggests that what is a threat to the ego is also, at the same time, a far more disturbing and fundamental predicament, indeed a predicament that may always prove "insoluble." What would it mean for a defensive process always to be "bound up with a splitting of consciousness [*Bewußtseinsspaltung*]" (SE 3: 48)? And what would it mean for the ego to live an insoluble predicament?

Crisis of Health

How is it, Freud will ask in "Neurosis and Psychosis" (1924), that the ego ever succeeds in not falling ill? If conflict is the condition of the ego, health, not pathology, arises as a question:

The statement that neuroses and psychoses . . . correspond to a failure [*Fehlschlagen*] in the functioning of the ego . . . this statement requires another discussion in order to be completed. One would like to know in what circumstances and by what means the ego can succeed [*gelingt*] in getting away [*entkommen*] from [its] conflicts, which are certainly always present, without falling ill. This is a new field of research, in which no doubt the most varied factors will have to be taken into account. (SE 10: 152)

From the opening lines of this short paper, it is clear that health depends on a balance of power between psychical agencies: "In my recently published work, *The Ego and the Id*, I have proposed a differentiation [*Gliederung*] of the mental apparatus on the basis of which a number of relationships can be represented in a simple and perspicuous manner" (SE 10: 149). The "differentiation" to which Freud refers here is the division of mind into three distinct yet inseparable agencies. These agencies are 1) the id (wholly unconscious and consisting of drives and repressed material), 2) the ego (partly conscious and containing the mechanisms of defense as well as the capacities to reason and to calculate), and 3) making its appearance at this date, the *superego* (also only partly conscious ruling the conscience and, beyond this, unconscious feelings of guilt). With his new topographical theory of mind in place, Freud finds himself in a position to reexamine the pathological states that were under discussion in "The Neuro-Pychoses of Defense," and he will focus once again on the ego's reactions to an incompatible reality and the difference in pathogenic effect that is occasioned by the ego's "choice of defense." Freud begins by putting forth a simple formula: "*neurosis is the result* [Erfolg] *of a conflict between the ego and its id, whereas psychosis is the analogous outcome of a similar disturbance in the relations between the ego and the external world*" (SE 10: 149). Although Freud will defend the formula in the end (by supplementing it), he admits that "there are certainly good grounds for being suspicious [*mißtrauisch*] of such simple solutions" (SE 10: 149). Indeed, as we will see, these solutions encounter a "Komplikation" in the form of the superego.

In the case of a neurosis, Freud tells us, the ego may refuse to accept a powerful instinctual impulse in the id, or it may refuse to help this impulse to find a motor outlet, or it may deny this impulse "the object at which it is aiming" (SE 10: 149–50). In so doing, the ego is "following the commands of its superego—commands which, in their turn, stem from influences in the real external world that have found representation [*Vertretung*] in the superego" (SE 10: 150). The ego represses the id in response to the commands of the superego whose strength in turn is determined by influences in the external world; the ego takes sides with these powers (*Mächte*) whose demands have more strength than the instinctual demands of the id. The superego, according to this model, serves as a kind of frontier-creature between the id and the external world; it mediates and negotiates passage between what lies inside and outside the psyche. With neurotic patients, Freud concludes, the ego subdues the id—it puts an end to the conflict—"in the service [*im Dienste*] of the superego and of reality" (SE 10: 150).

In cases of psychosis, on the other hand, the disturbance takes a much more extreme and striking form. The powers of repression have so little force in a psychosis, says Freud, that "the external world is not perceived at all, or the perception of it has no effect whatever" (SE 10: 150). In an acute hallucinatory confusion, Freud continues, not only does the ego refuse (*verweigert*) to accept new perceptions, it autocratically creates a new world according to the wishful impulses of the id. The powers whose demands had such strength in a neurosis are overwhelmed in the case of a psychosis. Thus in a psychosis one finds that delusion is "applied like a patch [*Fleck*] over the place where originally a rent [*Einriß*] had appeared in the ego's relation to the external world" (SE 3: 151). Where in neurosis the ego "remains true to its dependence on the external world," in psychosis the ego "*lets itself be overpowered by the id and thus torn away from reality* [vom Es überwältigen und damit von der Realität losreißen läßt]" (SE 10: 151).[4] The glory of success, in the case of a psychosis, belongs to the id.

However, Freud does not conclude with this simple distinction between neurotic and psychotic defenses. Instead, he adds the following:

> A complication [*Komplikation*] is introduced into this apparently simple situation, however, by the existence of the superego, which, through a link that is not yet transparent to us [*noch nicht durchschauter Verknüpfung*], unites in itself influences coming from the id as well as from the external world, and is, as it were, an ideal model for that at which all aspiration of the ego is aiming—a reconciliation of its multiple relations of dependence. The attitude [*Verhalten*] of the superego should be taken into account—which has not hitherto been done—in every form of psychical illness. (SE 10: 151–52)

This is quite an addition. Not only does it bring together and reconcile in a single agency both sides and sources of conflict for the ego, but what emerges is a link or a tie, a "nodal point," that is also a "knot [*Verknüpfung*]": something that is not yet transparent and whose very transparency remains in question. We are reminded of Freud's cautionary words at the very beginning of this essay. On the basis of his differentiation of the mental apparatus, Freud claims, "a series of relationships can be represented in a simple and perspicuous [*übersichtlicher*] manner" (SE 10: 149). But there are other things, he admits, that are not "übersichtlich," others points that are not clear or open to a synoptic overview: "for example, in what concerns the origin [*Herkunft*] and role of the superego—enough remains that is obscure and unsettled [*unerledigt*]" (SE 10: 149). Through a knot that resists both light and understanding, the superego, whose existence is a "complication,"[5] must be distinguished from the id, on the one hand, and from the external world, on the other. The very locatability of the superego is being called into question here; it is no longer something that can be located simply on the inside or the outside of the psyche but rather something that appears as the *effect* of this dichotomy itself. It is an internal externality, a foreign object within the psyche.

However, one might suspect from Freud's early study of the psycho-neuroses that the conflicts of the ego as they are described in Freud's perfunctory formula in "Neurosis and Psychosis" do not tell the whole story. Conspicuously absent from this formula, for example, is the "outcome" that would characterize the superego's conflict with the ego in which the superego overpowers the ego: a conflict in which the ego is overwhelmed not by the external world itself but by the agency that "play[s] the part" of the external world in the psyche (SE 23: 206). Indeed, ten years earlier, Freud had described the obsessional neurotic as one who suffered from a "super-morality" (SE 12: 325), and that very same year, in *The Ego and the Id*, he had studied cases both of obsessional neuroses and melancholia in which an "excessively strong" superego "rages against the ego with merciless violence" (SE 19: 54). We are all the more surprised therefore to find no discussion of this conflict and its outcome in an essay that reminds us that the superego "should be taken into account ... in every form of psychical illness." Freud will go so far as to mention the possibility of a conflict of this sort, but he does so guardedly, and only as an afterthought—"We may provisionally [*vorläufig*] assume that there must also be illnesses which are based on a conflict between the ego and the superego" (SE 10: 152). It is following this addendum that we find Freud raising the question of the possibility of health. How is it that the ego ever succeeds in not falling ill when the ego invariably falls into conflict with the id, the external world, and—perhaps also—the superego about whose origin and role "enough remains obscure and unelucidated"?

The question of health belongs to the future and to the future of research: "This is a new field of research, in which no doubt the most varied factors will have to be taken into account" (SE 10: 152). Freud cites two factors in particular whose significance, he speculates, will have to come up for future examination. Mentioning first the "economic considerations," which will "undoubtedly [*unzweifelhaft*]" (SE 10: 152) have to be taken into account in any psychical outcome, Freud comes to his second point:

> In the second place, it will be possible for the ego to avoid a break [*Bruch*] in any direction by deforming itself [*sich selbst deformiert*],

by consenting to losses [*Einbußen*] in its own unity, and eventually even by fissuring or dividing itself [*sich zerklüftet oder zerteilt*]. (SE 10: 152–53)

With this paradoxical claim, Freud is radically shifting the notion of splitting. In order to avoid a break, the ego must divide itself. In order not to lose itself, the ego must agree to lose its integrity. The ego saves itself by engaging in a preemptive strike. Deformation, loss of unity, self-fissuring, and self-division no longer "correspond to a failure in the functioning of the ego" but to the possibility of psychical health. The achievement of psychical health depends on a splitting of the ego.

If by "effecting a cleavage or division of itself" (SE 10: 153), by splitting itself, the ego avoids a pathogenic break, then the splitting of the ego can no longer be called "pathological." If, as Freud claims, it is possible for the ego "to avoid a break in any direction" by splitting itself, then there also exists—there must exist, says Freud—a mechanism by means of which the ego "detaches [*ablöst*] itself from the external world" (SE 10: 152–53) without falling ill.[6]

Crisis of Perception: The Splitting of the Ego

The question of ego splitting began to occupy Freud once again at the very end of his life. In *An Outline of Psychoanalysis*, written in 1938, in a chapter entitled "The Psychical Apparatus and the External World," Freud returns to the notion of a "psychical *split* [*psychische* Spaltung]" that occurs in the face of a reality that has become "intolerably painful [*unerträglich schmerzhaft*]" for the ego. But this time Freud will begin by explicitly challenging the line that separates the normal from the pathological: "We have seen that it is not scientifically feasible to draw a line of demarcation between what is psychically normal and abnormal" (SE 23: 195). In fact he will do more than challenge this line: he will claim to have "established the right [*das Anrecht begründet*]" to understand "the normal life of the mind from a study of its disorders" (SE 23: 195). This could not be done—it would not be "permissible [*nicht gestattet wäre*]" to posit such a right—were the specific causes of these pathological states (neuroses and psychoses) to operate solely from without, "in the manner of foreign bodies [*nach der Art von Fremdkörpern*]" (SE 23: 195).[7] In others words, the study of pathological ego splitting has provided Freud with the grounds for establishing the existence of non-pathological ego splitting.

THE NEW, THE STRANGE, AND THE FAMILIAR

The facts of ego splitting, writes Freud in the *Outline*, are "neither so new nor so strange [*nicht so neu und fremdartig*] as they may at first appear" (SE 23: 204). And yet, as he also writes, in a fragment dated the same year and entitled "Splitting of the Ego in the Process of Defense":

> I find myself for a moment in the interesting position of not knowing whether what I have to say should be regarded as something long familiar and self-evident or as something entirely new and puzzling [*längst bekannt und selbst-verständlich oder völlig neu und befremdend*]. (SE 23: 275)

The concept of "splitting"—elaborated in Freud's early work to explain the topographical difference between a neurotic and a psychotic reaction to an intolerable reality—has suddenly become "entirely new and puzzling." In Freud's early essays, psychical splitting designated a split between agencies: between the ego and the instinctual demands of the id on the one hand (neurosis), or between the ego and the external world on the other (psychosis). What is now being called a splitting of the ego, an "Ichspaltung," refers to an intra-systemic split, a split that divides or deforms the ego. By splitting itself, the ego neither represses (*verdrängt*) nor ejects (*verwirft*) an occurrence of incompatibility as it does in hysteria or psychosis. Instead, the ego maintains two contradictory attitudes *in consciousness* without the one influencing the other. It is this radical notion of ego splitting, a notion that challenges the very logic of consciousness, which leads Freud to posit a new defensive process: the process of disavowal.

Fetishism is certainly Freud's most famous example this process. But fetishism is only one example of disavowal. Indeed, in his discussion of fetishism, Freud points to another, more surprising example of disavowal in the case of obsessional neurosis. In what follows, we will see how Freud's 1927 essay on fetishism moves us from Wolfman to Ratman, from fetishism to obsessional neurosis, from a story of hallucinatory wish fulfillment to a real tragedy. I will show how, as a result of Freud's shift from fetishism to obsessional neurosis, the disavowal of sexual difference points to the disavowal of another reality entirely.

When Freud first uses the term "disavowal," it is in the context of the castration complex. It is used to describe the child's refusal to recognize the fact that women have no penis: children "disavow [*leugnen*] this absence and believe that they do see a penis" (SE 19: 143–44). The boy persistently endeavors to find himself or a mirror image of himself in others because he is unable to imagine "a person similar to himself without this important part," i.e. the penis (SE 19: 215–16). The girl, on the other hand, uses "disavowal" as a defense by refusing to acknowledge her lack of a penis. Freud concludes that this process—"which I should like to call a 'disavowal,' a process which in the mental life of children seems neither uncommon nor very dangerous . . . in an adult would mean the beginning of a psychosis" (SE 19: 252).

Not until the 1927 "Fetishism" essay does Freud make explicit the relation between disavowal and ego splitting. Freud begins with the example of the fetishist. The fetishist persists in the child's reaction to the perception of anatomical difference by holding two incompatible positions: he simultaneously perceives that a woman does not possess a penis *and* he refuses to acknowledge the fact of his perception. Both attitudes persist side by side throughout the life of the fetishist without influencing each other, resulting in a splitting of the ego. The fetishist's disavowal of the fact of feminine castration, Freud tells us, is not "scotomization"—it is not repression. This is because scotomization always refers to the creation of a blind spot. The term is particularly unsuited to the procedure of the fetishist, Freud explains, because it suggests that the incompatible reality (the absence of a penis) is "entirely wiped out, so that the result is the same as when a visual impression falls on the blind spot in the retina [*auf den blinden Fleck der Netzhaut*]" (SE 10: 153–54). In fetishism, on the contrary, the perception persists:

> The repudiation [*Ablehnung*] is always supplemented by an acknowledgment; two contrary and independent attitudes always arise and result in the situation of there being a splitting of the ego [*einer Ichspaltung*]. (SE 23: 204)

The fetishist sees and he does not see; he has acknowledged his perception and he has repudiated it. Like the child, he responds to the conflict with two contrary reactions, both of which are valid and effective [*giltig und wirksam*] (SE 23: 275). The fetishist has retained the belief that women have a penis, and he has given it up. The penis is no longer the same, however. Something else has taken its place. Something else has been appointed its substitute, something that inherits the interest that was formerly directed at its predecessor. In its defensive function, the fetish (like the dream) creates a "reality effect"; like the dream, the fetish functions as hallucinatory wish fulfillment (the fetishist sees what he wants to see). Freud cannot help but marvel at this solution. "One must admit," he confesses, that this is a "most ingenious [*geschickte*] solution to the difficulty."

In his unfinished and posthumous paper on the "Splitting of the Ego in the Process of Defense," Freud generalizes this account of ego splitting. Again the split occurs under the influence of a traumatic impression and again we find the ego caught between the demands of the id (the pleasure principle) and the prohibition of the external world. The ego must decide either to recognize the real danger, to give in to it and renounce an instinctual satisfaction, or "to disavow [*verleugnen*] reality and make itself believe that there is no reason for fear, so that it may be able to hold on to the satisfaction" (SE 23: 275). Again the ego's behavior is "remarkable [*merkwürdig*]" (SE 23: 275), and its way of dealing with reality "artful [*kniffig*]" (SE 23: 277). The ego decides neither in favor of the id nor in favor of reality, but instead takes both sides at once. Disavowal describes thus a paradoxical process in which *consciousness and perception* are used to defend *against* an intolerable reality. Precisely those things that give us reality are used to fend off reality.

But admiration is not Freud's final word on disavowal. In "Splitting of the Ego in the Process of Defense," as in his contemporaneous *Outline*, disavowal is not without remainder (*restlos*). Just as in Freud's earliest writings on neurosis and psychosis, psychological success comes at a cost. As we approach this most serious of topics, however, namely the cost of success, Freud once again adopts a idiom that is curiously flippant:

> Aber umsonst is bekanntlich nur der Tod ["Nothing is got for nothing," or literally: "But it is well known that only death is free of charge"]. Success [*Erfolg*] is achieved at the price of a rent [*Einriß*] in the ego that never heals but only gets larger with time. (SE 23: 275–76)

This new economy cannot be taken lightly. Freud himself will acknowledge the significance of the process he is describing. "The whole process"—in which two contrary responses to the psychical trauma "persist as the core of a splitting of the ego [*als Kern einer Ichspaltung bestehen bleiben*]"—"seems so strange [*sonderbar*] to us, because we hold the synthetic nature of the processes of the ego as self-evident [*weil wir die Synthese der Ichvorgänge für etwas Selbstverständliches halten*]" (SE 23: 276). We are "clearly wrong [*wir haben offenbar darin unrecht*]" to do this, for this synthetic function is subject to "particular conditions [*besonderen Bedingungen*]" and is "liable [*unterliegt*]"—vulnerable—to "a whole series of disturbances" (SE 23: 276). Perhaps it is our wrongness that must be taken lightly since our assumptions are so clearly off the mark. The synthetic function of the ego cannot be taken for granted. Indeed, the ego synthesizes with such compulsive force that Freud will often refer to the exigency to synthesize as a "Wißtrieb" (what Kant calls an "Erkenntnistrieb"): it is a *drive* that compels us to synthesis, even at the expense of reality. In the case of the child or the fetishist, on the contrary, "proper respect is shown to reality [*der gebührende Respekt gezollt worden ist*]" (SE 23: 275). Disavowal is always "supplemented [*ergänzt*]" (SE 23: 204) by an acknowledgment of reality. Two mutually exclusive attitudes are maintained in disavowal: "[t]he two contrary reactions to the conflict persist *as* the core of a splitting of the ego" (SE 23: 276, my emphasis). The whole process seems so strange to us, because the ego has literally become the moment or space of a splitting: two contradictory attitudes persist *as* core, as center, "als Kern." Could it be that the splitting of the ego *in* the process of defense (a pathology) repeats, as it were, a splitting of the ego *as* the process of defense (a necessity) ... such that the splitting of the ego remains both "new and puzzling" and "familiar and obvious"?

PRIMARY PROCESS

Indeed, one of Freud's earliest metapsychological notions reemerges from his discussion of disavowal. Disavowal, Freud tells us in 1927, is "only possible under the dominance of the unconscious laws of thought—*the primary process*" (SE 21: 154, my emphasis). Only a theory of primary process can explain and ground the possibility of disavowal. In his *Project for a Scientific Psychology* (1895) where the psyche is first described in terms of primary and secondary processes, Freud defines primary process as the wishful, hallucinatory revival of the memory of a previous satisfaction (SE 1: 326–27). Five years later, in Chapter 7 of *The Interpretation of Dreams* (1900), Freud will give a detailed account of primary process functioning when he evokes the familiar model of the hungry babe who hallucinates the breast.

The essential component of the infant's original experience of satisfaction (*Befriedigungserlebnis*) is a perception, "the memory image of which remains associated thenceforward with the memory-trace of the excitation produced by the need" (SE 5: 565). When next the infant is hungry, the same memory image is produced and perceived:

> [T]he reappearance of the perception is the fulfillment of the wish, and the shortest path to the fulfillment of the wish is one leading directly from the excitation produced by a need to a complete cathexis

of the perception. Nothing prevents us from assuming that there was a primitive state of the psychic apparatus in which this path was actually crossed, that is, in which wishing ended in hallucination. Thus, the aim of this first psychic activity was to produce a "perceptual identity [*eine Wahrnehmungsidentität*]"—a repetition of the perception linked [*verknüpft*] to the satisfaction of the need. (SE 5: 566)

Wishing does two things here: on the one hand, it replaces hunger with images of satisfaction; on the other hand, it prevents an investment in or cathexis of the painful experience itself. By eliminating the difference between memory and perception, wishing creates what Freud calls "a perceptual identity." The function of the perceptual experience in "a perceptual identity" is not perception, however. Rather perception becomes a sign of something else. It signals that an excitation produced by need (pain) has been replaced by an image linked to the satisfaction of this need (pleasure). The infant reproduces the perception that is linked to its prior satisfaction in order to recover a psychical state of rest (*psychischer Ruhezustand*).[8]

Like the dream, the infant's hallucination is a perceptual experience whose function is wish fulfillment. In both cases, the pleasure principle remains the regulating principle. The pleasure principle dominates primary mental processes and would dominate all mental processes were it not for "the exigencies of life [*die Not des Lebens*]" that force the psyche to develop an alternative, more expedient mode of operation. Without some inhibition of the primary process, in other words, the psyche would never learn to distinguish between the perceptual experience of hallucination and the reality of the external world.

"The bitter experience of life must have changed this primitive thought-activity into a more expedient secondary one" (SE 5: 566). From a perceptually closed, self-contained, self-sufficient regulating system, the infant is forced to acknowledge, confront, and judge a reality that inhibits its pleasure. This secondary thought-activity or "secondary process" is regulated by a new principle, the principle of reality. In Freud's hypothetical account of the beginning of the reality principle, it is "the non-appearance [*das Ausbleiben*]" of the expected satisfaction—the failure of the psyche to defend against an increase of tension by way of hallucinatory wish fulfillment (primary process)—that forces the psychical apparatus to change its defensive strategy. When wishing does not produce satisfaction, the psyche must find new ways of influencing the external causes of tension in order to change them in the desired manner.

This "inhibition" of the psyche's regressive tendencies to hallucinate becomes "the task of a second system" (SE 5: 566). "A new principle of mental functioning was thus introduced; what was presented in the mind was no longer what was agreeable but what was real, even if it happened to be disagreeable" (SE 12: 219).[9] Although secondary processes may indeed be distinguished from primary processes by the existence of an ego governed by considerations of safety and self-preservation, it would be a mistake to regard the defensive process as extraneous to the primary process. On the contrary, wish fulfillment and defense work together in the primary process: "[t]he wishful state results in a positive *attraction* towards the object wished for, or, more precisely, towards its mnemic image; the experience of pain leads to repulsion, a disinclination to keeping the hostile image cathected. Here we have primary *wishful attraction* and primary *defense*" (SE 1: 322).

Thus the primary process is never "primary" in the sense that it is ever simply succeeded or replaced by what Freud calls the "secondary process." Indeed, the impulses of the primary process persist in "our dreams at night and our waking tendency to tear ourselves away from distressing impressions" (SE 12: 219). And more fundamentally still for the purpose of this discussion, the "regressive" tendencies of the primary process persist as *disavowal*. In fetishism, as we have seen, disavowal serves to eliminate the "disagreeable" reality of genital difference. A fetish is created, and this creation makes reality agreeable once again. As a general process of *defense*, therefore, disavowal uses primary process wish fulfillment or fantasy, that is to say, *perception itself*, as a quasi-delusional corrective to an intolerable reality.

Insofar as the primary process constitutes a process of defense, it can be neither historically nor structurally first. Freud will curiously acknowledge as much in a footnote to his "Formulations on the Two Principles of Mental Functioning" (1911):

It will be rightly objected that an organization which was slave to the pleasure principle and neglected the reality of the external world could not maintain itself alive for the shortest time, so that it could not have come into existence at all. The employment of a fiction like this [*die Verwendung einer derartigen Fiktion*] is, however, justified when we consider that the infant, provided one includes with it the care it receives from its mother [*wenn man nur die Mutterpflege hinzunimmt*], does almost [*nahezu*] realize a psychical system of this kind. (SE 12: 220)

"[P]rovided" there is a supplemental inclusion, the infant "almost" realizes a psychical system of this kind. If the theoretical "fiction" of an organization ruled exclusively by the pleasure principle is necessary—if the theoretical "fiction" of an originary time of primary process functioning prior to the more expedient thought-activity of the secondary process is necessary—why is it necessary? Why is it necessary to maintain the primacy of primary process when Freud makes it clear that primary process must already include what is secondary? Primary process is not simply primary if, in order to be primary, the organization must fully realize a psychical system in which it either hallucinates itself to death or in which it must derive material sustenance from its hallucinations, which is impossible. Primary process, according to Freud, has indeed always failed to be "primary" in any historical sense: it is a "fiction." Freud's "provision," his "almost" are further concessions to this fiction. They register the knowledge of an unbridgeable gap between a necessary experience of satisfaction (perception) and the hallucination of satisfaction (memory). Insofar as there is hallucination, there has already been an unconscious perception of difference: there has been the registration and repudiation of a reality. For it is the non-correspondence between the present perception and the memory of satisfaction that gives rise to hallucination in the first place. To "almost" realize a self-sufficient psychical system is to acknowledge the dependence of the primary process (the very possibility of hallucinating the breast) on something that is not only not "secondary" but necessary—more primary, thus—to the "primary" process itself. This necessary dependence of the primary process, however, is also what makes primary process *primary*—as hallucinatory wish fullfilment or as first fiction. By failing to be "primary" in relation to "secondary" processes, primary process inscribes the original catastrophe of any psychical (or theoretical) system: the impossibility of realizing itself. In this way, primary process effectively testifies to a failure—its failure to be first—but this failure is, as Freud might say, "ein folgenschwerer Schritt," a momentous step, for it is nothing other than the failure to fend off what is "real": "what was presented in the mind was no longer what was agreeable but what was real" (SE 12: 219). "The real," says Freud, is always "that which resists recognition, not because it hides itself, but because it is that "which always remains 'unknowable [*unerkennbar*]'" (SE 23: 196).

The failure of primary process to defend against the "real" is a failure to defend against conscious thought activity or the "phenomenon of becoming conscious" (SE 18: 28). Conscious thought activity (that thought activity which is capable of verbalization) emerges from the disruption of perceptual identity. "Non-coincidence," says Freud, is what "gives the impulse for the activity of thought" (SE 1: 328). What this means, however, is that nothing can register the "non-coincidence" of primary and secondary processes because consciousness is itself this registration. "[C]onsciousness and memory are mutually exclusive," writes Freud in an early letter to Fliess in which he charts the development of consciousness (SE 1: 234). "[C]onsciousness arises instead of a memory-trace" (SE 18: 28). Thought activity is thus bound to the fiction of primary process. Primary process is "primary," one might say, not only because it is the first fiction, but because *as* fiction it tells another story of primacy. On the one hand, primary process is a process of hallucinatory wish fulfillment that has always failed to prevent the real from arriving. On the other hand, however, the primary process testifies to the *primacy* of the real—precisely by failing to be "primary."

PRIMARY DISAVOWAL

As hallucinatory wish fulfillment, fetishism creates a fantasy and a fiction. As defensive process, however, fetishism entertains a privileged relationship with reality (privileged because wholly conscious). Fetishism is not a neurosis. This is because disavowal succeeds too well in warding off the reality of genital difference. The creation of the fetish testifies to a reality that is not only effectively but also *perceptually* repudiated. As Freud tells us in the opening lines of "Fetishism," one should never expect fetishists to come to analysis "on account of their fetish [*des Fetish wegen*]" (SE 21: 152). "Usually they are quite satisfied with it, or even praise the way in which it eases their erotic life" (SE 21: 152).

Fetishism, as we have seen, is Freud's privileged example of the process of disavowal. The fetish is used to nullify and replace the woman's (the mother's) missing phallus. The woman must have a penis because if she is castrated then the possibility of castration is real. In this way, the creation of the fetish is the result of an intention "to destroy *the evidence for the possibility* of castration [den Beweis für die Möglichkeit *der Kastration zu zerstören*], so that fear of castration [can] be avoided" (SE 23: 203, my emphasis).

What cannot be tolerated by the fetishist is the "fact" of women's castration:

[T]he unwelcome fact of women's castration [*die unliebsame Tatsache der Kastration des Weibes*] is disavowed in fetishists. (SE 10: 156)

Freud is giving us the facts here. "Das sind die nackten Tatsachen," he is telling us, "these are the hard and cold facts." And yet, much has been written about the so-called "fact" of castration. Hundreds of pages have been devoted to Freud's inconsistency in claiming to talk about an oscillation between reality and fantasy when, in fact, he is describing the oscillation between two *fantasies*. Like the fetishist, it is claimed, Freud is here imposing a perception of fantasy on a perception of reality; he is using fantasy to cloak a disagreeable reality. However, like the strategy of the fetishist, there is something that deserves to be called "kniffig" or "artful" in Freud's way of handling "reality." As Jacques Lacan remarks, "it might be a good idea to re-examine the question by asking what could have imposed on Freud the obvious paradox of his position."[10] Could it not be said that Freud's account of phallic primacy (phallic monism) is itself the fetishization of a genital condition? Why, one must ask, should the feminine psyche be conditioned by the loss of something that was not lost, since it was never possessed?[11] In disavowal, Freud maintains that the attitude that fits in with reality and the attitude that fits in with fantasy persist simultaneously. If, then, the attitude that fits in with reality is itself a fantasy, and if the "divided attitude" of the fetishist (SE 10: 156) is an oscillation between two fantasies (castrated/not-castrated), then what the fetishistic structure of opposed fantasies disavows is another reality: a reality—I will suggest—far more distressing than sexual difference.[12] Indeed the oppositional structure of fetishism (the fantasy), which is here called "disavowal," succeeds *as* disavowal precisely because it does what it says. Castration *must* be considered a "fact," in other words, if "Fetishism" (the essay) is to illustrate the process of disavowal. Because Freud takes castration as a "fact," his essay becomes a form of disavowal.

We have already seen how the creation of a fetish destroys the "evidence for the possibility of castration." As that which substitutes for the missing penis, the fetish itself, whatever it may be (foot, shoe, fur, velvet, pieces of underclothing) remains "the sign of triumph [*das Zeichen des Triumphes*] over the threat of castration" and the protection against it (SE 10: 154). The "abhorrence at castration [*Abscheu vor der Kastration*]," Freud explains, sets up "a memorial [*ein Denkmal*] to itself in the creation of this substitute" (SE 10: 154). The fetish is a sign of triumph and a monument to abhorrence. Both sign and monument inscribe castration as a "fact." If this "fact" is fantasy, however, then what Freud is calling "fetishism" is not *disavowal* but what is here called "Fetishism" *is* disavowal. Or to raise the same question differently: what is the intolerable reality that is being disavowed by the essay?

FREUD'S OTHER EXAMPLE

> It is as if the parents said: You can certainly go away, but you must take us with you. (Anna Freud, *Psychoanalysis for Teachers and Parents*)

Fetishism, Freud acknowledges in the 1938 *Outline*, must lead beyond fetishism:

> It must not be thought that fetishism presents an exceptional case as regards a splitting of the ego; it is merely a particularly favorable object of study for it. Let us return to our thesis that the childish ego, under the domination of the real world, gets rid of unpleasant instinctual demands by what are called repressions [*Verdrängungen*]. We will now supplement this by the further assertion that... the ego often enough finds itself in the position of fending off some demand from the external world which it feels distressing, and that this occurs by means of a *disavowal* [Verleugnung] of the perceptions which bring to knowledge this demand from reality. Disavowals of this kind occur very often and not only with fetishists. (SE 23: 203–04)

> Whatever the ego does in its efforts of defense [*Abwehrbestreben*], whether it seeks to disavow [*verleugnen*] a portion of the real external world or whether it seeks to reject [*abweisen*] an instinctual demand from the internal world, its success [*Erfolg*] is never complete and without remainder [*restlos*]. The outcome always lies in two contrary attitudes (SE 23: 204).

These passages astonish critics far too little, for Freud is not only distinguishing between the terms "repression" and "disavowal," he is also rethinking the central position of repression in psychoanalysis. The center, which was once repression, has shifted by admitting an alternative between defensive strategies ("whether it seeks to disavow ... or whether it seeks to reject"). The center, one might say, is now split between disavowal of the external world on the one hand and repression of the internal world on the other.[13] So how are we to read this split? What is the reality at stake in this rethinking of one of the fundamental postulates of psychoanalysis?

To begin to answer these questions, let us return for a moment to Freud's own conclusions about the theoretical interest of disavowal in his "Fetishism" essay:

> For me, the explanation of fetishism held yet another theoretical interest. Recently, along purely speculative lines, I arrived at the proposition that the essential difference between neurosis and psychosis was in that

in the former the ego, in the service of reality, suppresses a piece of the id, whereas in a psychosis it lets itself be induced [*sich fortreißen lasse*] by the id to detach itself [*sich zu lösen*] from a piece of reality. But soon after this I had cause to regret that I had ventured so far. In the analysis of two young men I learned that both had failed to take cognizance of the death of their beloved father (one when he was two and the other when he was ten)—had "scotomized" it—and yet neither of them had developed a psychosis. (SE 10: 155–56)

Further research led to another solution.... It turned out that the two young men had no more "scotomized" their father's death than a fetishist does the castration of women. It was only one current [*Strömung*] in their mental life that had not recognized their father's death; there was another current which took full account of this fact [*Tatsache*]. The attitude which fitted in with the wish and the attitude which fitted in with reality [*die wunschgerechte wie die realitätsgerechte Einstellung*] existed side by side. In one of my two cases this split [*Spaltung*] had become the foundation [*Grundlage*] of a moderately severe obsessional neurosis. The patient oscillated [*schwankte*] in every situation in life between two assumptions [*Voraussetzungen*]: the one, that his father was still alive and hindering his activities [*seine Tätigkeit behindere*]; and the opposite one, that he had the right [*das Recht*] to consider himself the successor [*Nachfolger*] of his dead father. (SE 10: 156)

The sons have not repressed their father's death; they have disavowed it. Just as the fetishist knows and does not know that the woman has no penis, the sons who disavow their father's death know and do not know their father is dead. The two kinds of knowledge persist side by side without influencing each other. In fetishism, what is defended against is the intolerable threat of women's castration, and the fetish provides a positive hallucination of phallic presence. Here, on the other hand, what is being disavowed is the death of a father.

In one of the sons, however, this disavowal has led to a moderately severe obsessional neurosis. What is more, the "wunschgerechte" attitude of this son is immediately complicated by ambivalence: alive, his father is a hindering presence. One cannot help but wonder whether it is indeed the father's *death* that this son is disavowing? Does the son want to be hindered in his activities? Ambivalence is a complication. And this complication is difficult to contain: not only is ambivalence present in the son's "wunschgerechte" attitude, but it infects his "realitätsgerechte" attitude as well and begins to blur the boundaries between both currents of his mental life.

Even when the son takes full account of the fact of his father's death, that is to say, when he recognizes what is not recognized in one current of his mental life, we find him asserting his "right" of succession. Is this right one that is being contested? To succeed a *dead* father, after all, is to beat a dead horse. Who or what is preventing the son from living, from becoming the "Nachfolger" of his dead father? Why is this son unable to put his father's death to rest? This incapacity is precisely what Freud is calling "obsessional neurosis."

Freud's study of obsessional neurosis will in fact address the problem of the ego's inability to live unhindered in its activities. Let us turn therefore to Freud's analysis of this crazy illness and to the strange reality of the undead father.

A Crazy Illness

> What it is it that the ego fears from the external and from the libidinal danger of the id cannot be specified; we know that it is an overpowering or an annihilation [*Überwältigung oder Vernichtung*], but it cannot be grasped analytically. (SE 19: 60)

PRESENTATION OF THE ILLNESS

"Obsessional neurosis [*die Zwangsneurose*]," says Freud, "is unquestionably the most interesting and rewarding subject [*wohl das interessanteste und dankbarste Objekt*] of analytic research, but as a problem it is still unmastered [*unbezwungen*]" (SE 20: 113). Although obsessional neurosis was one of the illnesses upon whose study psychoanalysis was first built, it never became as popular as "the universally familiar hysteria" because it was not "so obtrusively noisy" and behaved more like "a private affair" (SE 16: 258).[14] What so astonishes Freud about obsessional neurosis is its absurdity:

Certainly this is a crazy illness [*ein tolles Leiden*]. The most extravagant psychiatric imagination would not, I think, have succeeded in constructing anything like it; and if one did not see it before one every day one would never bring oneself to believe in it. Do not suppose, however, that you can help the patient in the least by calling on him to take a new line, to cease to occupy himself with such foolish thoughts and to do something sensible instead. . . . He would like to do so himself, for he is completely clear in his head, shares your opinion of his obsessional symptoms and even puts it forward to you spontaneously. Only he cannot help himself. What is carried into action in an obsessional neurosis is sustained by an energy to which we probably know nothing comparable in normal mental life. (SE 16: 259)

Obsessional neurosis is characterized by patients who are occupied with thoughts that do not interest them, who are troubled by strange and disturbing impulses, and who are compelled against their will to perform actions that give them no pleasure. Although these actions (compulsions) are in themselves harmless and trivial things—repetitions or ceremonial elaborations of the activities of ordinary life (washing, dressing, or cleaning)—in the end they become extremely tedious and almost insoluble tasks. The obsessional patient seems driven by an absolute and incomprehensible force to play out the drama of Luther's confession: "I cannot do otherwise, in spite of everything."[15] In this context, Freud will speak of the "unwritten laws" and sacrality of obsessive actions (SE 9: 118). Any deviation from the obsessive ritual is visited by such intolerable anxiety that it is impossible for the patient not to act. The obsessional patient behaves like a person possessed.[16] What possesses the obsessional neurotic, however, is a very peculiar force of obligation that resembles nothing so much as a "super-morality" (SE 5: 251). Obsessional neurosis, says Freud, is a strangely "moral illness," distinguished above all by hyper-conscientiousness, constant fear of temptation, intense self-reproach, and shame way beyond the demands of the normal superego. It is as if a taboo had already been violated and produced an unconscious, fearful sense of guilt (SE 13: 68); as if the ego of the obsessional neurotic were beset by a punishing conscience whose command knew no reprieve.

As we saw in fetishism, the fetishist bends perceptual data to his needs and maintains a desired sameness—"He wants to see the same in other people..." (SE 19: 142–43). But where the unwelcome perception of the fetishist finds symbolic erasure in the fetish and results in a splitting of the ego, the splitting of the ego in the case of the son's obsessional neurosis is not the symptom but the foundation of his illness—"this split had formed the basis [*die Grundlage*] of a moderately severe obsessional neurosis" (SE 21: 156). Obsessional neurosis is, in the case of one of the sons, a response to the splitting of the ego; one might say it is the example of pathological disavowal. To what extent, one may ask, does obsessional neurosis *take up* the story of ego splitting? And what might Freud's shift to obsessional neurosis tell us about the nature of the reality that has been disavowed from the very beginning?

TECHNIQUES OF THE ILLNESS

The revival of the term "defense" in 1926[17] corresponds to certain discoveries made by Freud in his study of the obsessional neuroses:

> Our first observations of repression and symptom formation were made in connection with hysteria. We saw that the perceptual content of exciting experiences and the representational content of pathogenic structures of thought were forgotten and barred [*ausgeschlossen*] from being reproduced in memory, and we therefore concluded that the keeping away [*Abhaltung*] from consciousness was a main characteristic of hysterical repression. Later on, when we came to study the obsessional neuroses, we found that in that illness pathogenic occurrences are not forgotten. They remain conscious but they are "isolated [*isoliert*]" in some way that we cannot as yet grasp.... Our attention has, moreover, been drawn to... a procedure, that may be called magical, of "making unhappened [*Ungeschehenmachen*]"—a procedure about whose defensive purpose there can be no doubt, but which has no longer any resemblance to the process of "repression." (SE 20: 163–64)

The technique of isolation is characteristic of obsessional neurosis, Freud tells us. In hysteria, the "traumatic impression" is repressed and lapses into amnesia (SE 20: 120). In obsessional neurosis, the experience is neither repressed nor forgotten, but it is stripped of its affect and separated from its associative relations so that the experience remains, as it were, "isolated." Freud's attention, however, is drawn to yet another procedure, one "that may be called magical" and "about whose defensive purpose there can be no doubt." This procedure, Freud says, has a wide range of applications and it goes very far back:

> It is, as it were, negative magic, and endeavors, by means of motor symbolism, to "blow away [*wegblasen*]" not only the consequences of an event (an impression or experience) but the event itself. I choose the term "blow away" advisedly,[18] so as to remind the reader of the part played by this technique not only in neuroses but in magical acts, popular customs and religious ceremonies as well.... This endeavor to make unhappen [*das Streben zum Ungeschehenmachen*] shades off into normal behavior in the case in which a person decides to treat an event as '*non arrivé*,' but whereas the normal person undertakes nothing against the event, and simply pays no further attention to it or its consequences, the neurotic person seeks to cancel out the past itself [*aufheben*]. (SE 20: 119–20)

Disavowal involves a compulsion to repeat. "What did not happen in the desired way is made unhappened [*ungeschehen gemacht*] by being repeated in a different way" (SE 20: 120). In the endeavor to make something unhappened, the normal person decides to treat an occurrence as "non arrivé." What we find in the case of obsessive undoing, it would seem, is a *literalization* of what the normal person does. It is as if the obsessional neurotic were reading the "as" of "*als* 'non arrivé'" not as "*as if*"—in the way the normal person does—but as an absolute equivalence; an intolerable event must be treated as an event that did not arrive: it never happened.

The normal person will take no direct action against the event. The obsessional neurotic is, in some real sense, too direct, too literal. What has already happened must be made unhappened: the impossible must be made possible. One is reminded here of the predicament of the ego as Freud described it in 1896: "the task that the ego, in its defensive attitude, sets itself of treating the incompatible representation as '*non arrivée*' is for the ego simply insoluble [*direkt unlösbar*]" (SE 3: 48). It is as if the obsessional neurotic were recognizing a new impossibility and a new imperative in the ego's predicament: not only must a task that is "direkt unlösbar" be made soluble, but it must now be made "direkt lösbar," not only soluble but soluble *directly*. In attempting to make unhappened what has already happened, the obsessional neurotic is once again drawn into a conflict that is actually insoluble. This time, however—although the task of making unhappened falls to the ego—the injunction comes from the superego. For the ego of the obsessional neurotic shares the analyst's view of his illness: "he is completely clear in his head, shares your opinion of his obsessional symptoms and even puts it forward to you spontaneously." The ego has and has not lost its autonomy; it is, as it were, bonded to its superego. The paradox that makes obsessional neurosis possible is, thus, a literalization of a normal process of differentiation. Where the ego has failed once, one might say, the superego must try to fail better.

ANOTHER MONUMENT

In the case of the fetishist, the fetish serves as a defense against the fear of castration. In the case of the son's disavowal of his father's death, however, what is it that the ego fears? Is it castration? Freud himself will raise this question: "Is it absolutely certain that fear of castration is the only motive force of . . . defense?" (SE 20: 123). Before this question can be answered, however, castration anxiety finds its "extension [*Fortbildung*]" in moral anxiety:

> Just as the father has become depersonalized [*unpersönlich*] in the superego, so has the fear of castration at his hands become transformed into an undefined social fear or a fear of conscience [*Gewissensangst*]. (SE 20: 128)

With depersonalization, however, comes a danger that is "less defined [*unbestimmter*]" (SE 20: 139). "Castration anxiety develops into moral anxiety [*Gewissensangst*]," but it is "no longer so easy to say what the anxiety fears [*was die Angst befürchtet*]" (SE 20: 139). With the "installation" (*Aufrichtung*) of the superego, the ego has both depersonalized the father and repersonalized its fear:[19] hence the superego "observes the ego, gives it orders, judges it and threatens it with punishments" (SE 23: 205). The superego is a tribunal, a court of appeals (*Instanz*). It is an "agency [*Instanz*]" true to its name. In the final pages of *The Ego and the Id*, in a chapter entitled "The Dependent Relationships of the Ego," Freud notes that "[a]mong the dependent relationships in which the ego stands, that to the superego is surely the most interesting" (SE 19: 59).

"The superego owes [*verdankt*] its special position in the ego, or in relation to the ego" (SE 19: 48) to its duel heritage. On the one hand, it is "the expression of the most powerful impulses and most important libidinal vicissitudes of the id"—it is "heir [*der Erbe*]" (SE 19: 36) to the early conflicts of the ego with the id, heir to the original narcissism of the child (SE 14: 94). On the other hand, the superego is the installation of the prohibition of the father in or in relation to the ego: it is "heir [*der Erbe*] to the Oedipus complex" (SE 19: 32).[20] The superego represents thus both the desired ideal toward which the ego strives and the injunction prohibiting its attainment: the superego's relation to the ego, says Freud, is not only not exhausted by the precept—"'You *ought to be* like this (like your father)'"—but also determined in its articulation by the very object of desire "'You *may not be* like this (like your father)'" (SE 19: 34). In other words, the superego is the entombment of an irreconcilable libidinal conflict.

Representing both the earliest object choices of the id and at the same time "an energetic reaction formation against these choices" (SE 19: 30), the superego fortifies the ego so that it may resist the pleasure principle (i.e. internal stimuli) and survive its trauma. The pleasure principle fuels the destructive force behind the libidinal vicissitudes of the id, which, if left to itself, would "murder even for trifles" (SE 14: 297). Were it not for the strength the ego received from elsewhere, in other words, the ego would have succumbed to the pleasure principle. Had the ego not borrowed strength to overcome the pleasure principle from "the father," had the ego not received strength on "loan" (SE 19: 30), the very concept of the ego would not have survived the despotism of the pleasure principle. Thus it is this event, this occurrence, this moment, this act of borrowing and lending—this loan—that is of such extraordinary consequence:

> [T]his loan [*diese Anleihe*] was an extraordinarily momentous act [*ein außerordentlich folgenschwerer Akt*]. (SE 19: 30)

However, this is not Freud's last word on the superego's relation to the ego. Not only does the superego have the capacity to master the ego, it remains "the memorial [*das Denkmal*] to the former weakness and dependence of the ego" (SE 19: 49). Like the creation of that other "memorial"—the fetish—*abhorrence* at the ego's former weakness and dependence sets up a memorial to itself in the creation of the superego.[21] The fetishist creates a substitute for the missing penis, that is to say, a fetish. In so doing, he has "disavowed reality, but he ha[s] saved his own penis" (SE 23: 277). The ego creates a substitute for the father in the superego. By setting up the superego, the ego disavows its former weakness but saves itself. The superego, like the fetish, is both a sign of triumph and a monument to abhorrence. As was the case in fetishism, the ego memorializes in order to forget.

And the ego (partially) succeeds in its task. By installing the superego, the ego has in some sense acknowledged a difference or alterity, a non-ego (whether we call this "the father," "the mother," or "the law"). However, this acknowledgement is marked by ambivalence. Indeed, by internalizing the relationship to the father in its relationship to the superego, the ego has in some real, bodily sense incorporated or devoured (cannibalized) the father. On the one hand, therefore, the installation of superego embodies the ego's attempt to incorporate the external world, that is, to destroy it. In its narcissistic striving to recover the same, the ego cannot help but follow the dedifferentiating path of the pleasure principle. Difference is always recuperated or reinscribed within the ego's psychical system as *self*-difference.

On the other hand, however, the installation of the superego creates a "differentiation" or differential structure within the ego (SE 19: 34). This differential structure can never be reduced to a pure self-identity, moreover, for the very installation of the superego (or ego ideal) memorializes the ego's failure to save its self. The superego is always an interiorization, an inclusion, in view of a compromise solution, but it also a heterogeneous space within the ego. The relation of the superego to the ego is therefore a relation of "third person" to "first person":

> The "third person," linguistically and psychically, as Benveniste has observed, is distinguished from the second precisely by being a "non-person," irreducible to the self-identity of an ego. . . . The third person therefore does merely join the first and second to form a trio of individuals, of egos: its presence marks the constitutive dependence of the ego on something that can never be fully assimilated to any form of self-identity. The "prohibition" that this third person installs—*aufrichtet*— does not, therefore, come upon the subject from without: it dislocates (*entstellt*) it from within, as it were, turning it inside-out, turning the "ego" outwards toward the superego.[22]

To the extent that the relation of the superego to the ego is determined by the grammatical or formal difference between "third person" and "first person," one would have to say that alterity or difference is registered not *in* the superego (whatever its social and cultural content) but *by* the superego. The emergence of the superego (its Faktum) registers an unassimilable difference that the ego itself has as its insoluble task to assimilate. And there is no reason why we should not call this insoluble task life, for it cannot be opposed to life.

By incorporating the father and saving itself, thus, the ego always exposes itself to a danger.[23] Indeed, the superego enters the scene not because the ego somehow wills its own indebtedness, but, on the contrary, because it is only by incorporating the father that the ego can survive the father. In normal cases, that is to say, most of the time, this incorporation of the father occasions little or no upset. In the case of the obsessional neurotic, on the other hand, incorporation results in digestive failure (though it would be equally true to say that what is indigestible is bound to cause internal distress). The obsessional neurotic, one might say, fails to incorporate and depersonalize the father.

Enough remains that is obscure and unsettled, Freud tells us, in what concerns the superego (SE 10: 149). The superego is heir to the Oedipus complex and is only established after that complex has been dissolved. And Freud adds: "This reminds us that the hero of the Oedipus legend too felt guilty for his deeds and submitted himself to self-punishment, although the coercive power of the oracle should have acquitted him of guilt in our judgment and his own" (SE 23: 205). How are we to read the legacy of Oedipus here? Is the hero of the Oedipus legend an obsessional whose sadistic superego torments and punishes him excessively? Ironically, I will suggest, the story of Oedipus is extremely helpful, for it provides a literal and literary model for Freud's obsessional patient.[24] Oedipus, we must remember, has two fathers: Laïus of Thebes, his biological father whom he unwittingly kills at a crossing (the original "Oedipal" father who is killed and returns as the Law), and the childless Polybus of Corinth, Oedipus's adoptive father, who raises Oedipus and lives until a ripe old age. It is literally true, in other words, that Oedipus kills his father and that he does not kill his father, that his father is dead and not dead. Could it be, then, that the disavowal that forms the basis of the son's moderately severe obsessional neurosis in "Fetishism" is forever trying to undo the past because something crucial, some crucial reality has been missed—not the Oedipal father who has been repressed, but the other father, the father who cannot be murdered?

Indices of Difference

> These considerations clear the way for the following question: does disavowal [*Verleugnung*]—whose consequences *in* reality are so obvious— not point to a factor that founds human reality rather than to a hypothetical "fact of preception"? (Laplanche and Pontalis, *The Language of Psychoanalysis*)

The disavowal that forms the groundwork of the son's obsessional neurosis oscillates between an either/or that cannot be resolved to the ego's satisfaction:

> The patient oscillated [*schwankte*] in every situation in life between two assumptions: the one, that his father was still alive and hindering his activities; and the opposite one, that he had the right [*das Recht*] to consider himself the successor [*Nachfolger*] of his dead father. (SE 10: 156)

In disavowing the death of his father, the son is also disavowing his right to live unhindered by his father. Instead of a father who has become "depersonalized in the superego" (SE 20: 128), we have a dead father who refuses to die, a dead father whose "existence" exceeds all ontological oppositions between absence and presence, visible and invisible, living and dead, a dead father whose "existence" resists the ego's greatest efforts at depersonalization.

In the final lines of the 1938 *Outline*, Freud quotes Goethe on the discontinuous nature of successions: "Was du ererbt von deinen Vätern hast, Erwirb es, um es zu besitzen" (What you have inherited from your fathers, acquire it to make it yours) (SE 23: 207). Freud is not quoting these lines for the first time. In *Totem and Taboo*, he quotes them in the context of the psychical heritage between generations. When he quotes them again in the *Outline*, the context is that of the relation between the present and the past of an individual. Both times, however, the question of succession arises as a problem of discontinuity. In the case of what Freud calls an "inheritance of psychical dispositions" in *Totem and Taboo*, there must occur in the life of the individual some sort of impetus or trigger before the latter's dispositions "can be roused into actual operation" (SE 13: 158). Continuity between generations is not a given; rather it must be initiated by an event. In the second case, Freud contends that the superego "unites in itself the influences of the present and the past" (SE 23: 207). Because of its dual heritage, the superego "takes up a kind of intermediate position between the id and the external world" (SE 23: 207).

Thus, for the normal person the superego "continues to play [*zu spielen*] the part of an external world for the ego, although it has become a portion of the internal world" (SE 23: 206). In the case of Freud's obsessional patient, on the other hand, the superego has failed to play its part. It has failed to assume its "role [*Rolle*]." The superego has literally remained an externality: it remains an instance that repels any depersonalization by the ego. What remains tolerable as a process of "differentiation" in the case of a normal person might be termed a "splitting" in the case of the obsessional neurotic. However this "splitting" is no longer a splitting of the ego, unless by splitting one understands shipwreck, for the ego can no longer help itself here. For the first time, in other words, something other than ego has emerged: neither ego nor superego but something wholly unrelated to ego, and which may perhaps be called, at least in the case of Freud's patient, "a traumatic bond." A traumatic bond is what remains; it is that absolute difference which the process of disavowal cannot reach but which forms the basis of the son's obsessional neurosis. Unlike self-difference or depersonalization, absolute difference cannot be made compatible with the ego because the ego is itself wholly constituted against it. Only the obsessional neurotic, it would seem, is able to register the real difference of absolute difference. Fortunately, one might add, because it is an intolerable difference.

Freud's shift from fetishism to obsessional neurosis points to the disturbing and fundamental nature of the mechanism of disavowal and suggests that the history of psychoanalysis may have unwittingly repressed an insight into the most revolutionary notion of otherness. One might say that Freud's concept of disavowal is itself split between a fantasy of disavowal on the one hand (fetishism) and the reality of disavowal on the other (obsessional neurosis). We have seen how, in the creation of the fetish, memorialization is bound up with forgetting. Thus the fetish—"usually," "as a rule," (SE 21: 152)—testifies to an encounter with a difference that is not only effectively but perceptually repudiated. For the normal person, the installation of the superego is successfully recuperated by the ego as the indispensable and irreducible other *of the ego*. And yet the notion of difference as a difference that can be disavowed by hallucinatory wish fulfillment (sexual difference) or forgotten by the ego in its memorialization (the Oedipal father) is dependent on and derived from another notion of difference in which difference functions as absolute primacy that allows for no symbolic mediation whatsoever. Absolute difference would stand above and beyond all perceptual difference in its primacy, or, I would argue, in its positional power of difference.

But the disavowal of Freud's obsessional patient in "Fetishism" also returns us to an earlier structure of impossibility—that of the necessary failure of the primary process—from which thought activity itself emerges. One might say that obsessional neurosis carries us back to "reality." However, this return as obsessional neurosis suggests that what was originally the emergence of consciousness is not without an ethical dimension. We have seen how the disavowal of Freud's obsessional patient issues in a radical notion of otherness, an otherness that no longer corresponds to the pseudo-moral instance of the superego, but rather points to the absolute difference of the undead father from which/whom the son cannot break free. Indeed, it would be this indenture that testified to "reality" not simply as thought activity (the traumatic-pre-traumatic) but as traumatic bond or debt. What is intolerable, it would seem, is the relationship to an external reality whose force or power remains utterly *unresponsive to the ego.* And yet without this irreducible, traumatizing force, there would be nothing in the world to move us beyond the pleasure principle. Thus, it is the study of obsessional neurosis, the study of this "crazy illness" that leads Freud to conclude that the human psyche "is not only far more immoral than [it] believes but also far more moral than [it] knows" (SE 19: 53). The bond to absolute difference, from which we never recover, is, it would seem, the price we pay for moral possibility: a moral possibility that is irreducible to the ego and to the ego's conflicts with the pleasure principle. The tragedy is that this possibility is one the obsessional neurotic above all would prefer to forget.

§3 Flaubert

Testament to Disaster

Que nuist sçavoir tousjours et tousjours apprendre, feust ce
d'un sot, d'un pot, d'une guedoufle, d'une moufle, d'une
pantoufle?

— (Rabelais, *Le Tiers Livre*)

Introduction

THE LEGACY OF ROMANTICISM

No writer has seen his name more linked to a concept he de-
tested than Gustave Flaubert. From the moment of the publication
of *Madame Bovary* in 1857, literary history has hailed Flaubert as
the father, "founder, chief practitioner and high priest" of *realism*.[1]
And yet—not only did the thought of paternity horrify Flaubert[2]—
nothing was more galling to him than theories, systems, schools
of thought that made pronouncements and allegations about the
world: "Peignons, peignons, sans faire de théorie" (Let us paint,
paint without building theories) (CB 2: 209); "je n'aime les doctrinaires d'aucune espèce.... Loin de moi ceux qui se prétendent
réalistes, naturalistes, impressionistes...moins de paroles et plus
d'œuvres!" (I do not like doctrinaires of any kind...Away those
who claim to be realists, naturalists, impressionists...less talk and
more works!). To Edma Roger des Genettes, he even claimed that
Madame Bovary was conceived wholly out of a "hatred [*haine*]" of
realism (CB 2: 643). Indeed more than twenty years later, Flaubert
is still raving against realism: "Et notez que j'exècre ce qu'on est
convenu d'appeler le *réalisme*, bien qu'on me fasse un de se pon-
tifes" (and note that I loathe what is called *realism*, even though
they make me out to be one of its pontiffs) (GS 521); "Ne me parlez

pas du réalisme, du naturalisme, ou de l'expérimental! J'en suis gorgé. Quelles vides inepties!" (Do not speak to me of realism, naturalism or the experimental! I am fed up with them. What empty nonsense!) (GM 199). Flaubert's lifelong antipathy to the concept of "realism" stems from a fundamental aversion—both aesthetic and moral[3]—to theories that claim to make sense of the world.

However, and from the outset, Flaubert himself must readily concede that *Madame Bovary* no longer conforms to the lyrical, romantic tradition of French writers. To Sainte-Beuve who has recently praised *Madame Bovary* in a long article for *Le Moniteur*,[4] Flaubert insists that despite *Madame Bovary* he himself still belongs—"par le cœur du moins"—to an earlier generation of writers:

> Je voudrais bien cependant vous éclairer sur un point tout *personnel*. Ne me jugez pas d'après ce roman. Je ne suis pas de la génération dont vous parlez—par le cœur du moins. —Je tiens à être de la vôtre, j'entends de la bonne, celle de 1830. Tous mes amours sont là. Je suis un vieux romantique enragé, ou encroûté, comme vous voudrez.
>
> Ce livre est pour moi une affaire d'art pur et de parti pris.[5] Rien de plus. D'ici à longtemps je n'en referai de pareils. Il m'a été *physiquement* pénible à écrire. Je veux maintenant vivre (ou plutôt revivre) dans des milieux moins nauséabonds. (CB 2: 710)

> But allow me enlighten you on a purely *personal* point. Do not judge me by this book. I do not belong to the generation of which you speak—in my heart at least. —I insist that I belong to yours, I mean the good generation, that of 1830. Everything I love is there. I am a rabid old romantic, or a crusty old one, if you prefer.
>
> I regard this book as a work of pure art and bias. Nothing more. It will be a long time before I write anything else of the kind. It was *physically* painful for me to write. Now I want to live (or rather resume living) in a less putrid environment.

"[É]pris de *gueulades*, de lyrisme, de grands vols d'aigle, de toutes les sonorités de la phrase et des sommets de l'idée" (enamored of declamation, lyricism, great eagle flights, every tone of phrase and lofty ideas) (CB 2: 30), Flaubert belongs *in his heart* to the generation of Chateaubriand and Victor Hugo. The flamboyance of his early works, and particularly his first *Tentation de Saint Antoine*, has often led critics to speak of Flaubert as a "second generation romantic." Moreover, there are his letters—the confessional musings in which Flaubert recalls his penchant for lyrical exuberance. He is, he writes, a male hysteric whose most natural expression is hyperbole: "Moi!—débris d'un monde disparu, vieux fossile du romantisme!" (Me!—the wreckage of a lost world, an old fossil of romanticism!) (IT 102); " . . . moi qui ai couché la tête sur un poignard" (I who slept with a dagger beneath my head) (IT 74), "qui suis *un vieux romantique*" (who am *an old romantic*) (GS 80), "une *âme* incomprise . . . le seul survivant de la vieille race des Troubadours!" (a misunderstood spirit . . . the sole survivor of the old race of Troubadours!) (S 3: 317). Nothing could be further from Flaubert's heart it would seem, than the writing of *Madame Bovary*. He is not, he feels compelled to clarify, " *ce* roman," "[*c*]*e* livre"—and one might add " *cette* affaire d'art pur et de parti pris"—those things to which he points and which fill him with disgust. *Madame Bovary*, he is telling Sainte-Beuve, ce n'est pas moi—"par le cœur du moins."

For Flaubert (who was born in 1821), Romanticism is not only a cultural heritage: it is also his immediate and personal past. To refer to the generation of the French romantics as Flaubert does is to evoke the preceding generation in whose waning he cannot help but participate. In fact, the name "Flaubert" actually marks the place in literary history where Romanticism comes to an end. What would it mean for Flaubert to be an "old romantic" under these conditions? What would it mean for Romanticism to live on in Flaubert?

I will argue in what follows that what Proust calls "le style de Flaubert" (the narrating, analyzing, pathos-less machine, the unrelenting force of indifferentiation that is Flaubert) forces us to read, on the level of grammar and syntax, an obdurate futurity that lies at the "heart" of Romanticism. In the name of Romanticism, precisely against it in its name, Flaubert's style ushers in a new temporality—a temporality of the future. Paradoxically, in other words, only by sacrificing his heart, his old romantic heart, can Flaubert rigorously convey what is the non-romantic essence of romantic temporality.[6] Flaubert's romantic heritage emerges, thus, in the very writing of *Madame Bovary*—in a writing so detached from the woman it portrays that "five generations of critics have not yet been able to decide whether [Flaubert] likes her or not."[7] If "romanticism" tells us something about the world, therefore, it is not, as Flaubert's writing suggests, because it reflects or tries to reflect reality, but because it carries with it a dimension of futurity that no "realism" as such is able to reach.

THE MOVING WALKWAY

Nowhere does the difficulty of reading the revolutionary force (indeed the futurity) of Flaubert arise more clearly and vociferously than in the famous controversy that takes place in the pages of *La Nouvelle Revue Française* between Marcel Proust and Albert Thibaudet. In this debate, which illustrates the problem of humanistic readings of literature in general, the difficulty of reading the "human" in Flaubert emerges precisely as a question of style.

The controversy arises as a result of an article published by Albert Thibaudet, "Le style de Flaubert," in which he argues that Flaubert is not what one might call "un écrivain de race [*a writer of distinction*]."[8] Were it not for Flaubert's "fiery temperament" and his "Norman obstinacy," Thibaudet contends, Flaubert's style might never have overcome its natural indigence.[9]

In his brilliant 1920 article "À propos du 'style' de Flaubert," written in response Thibaudet's article, Proust immediately takes issue with this characterization of Flaubert's style. Whatever Flaubert's personal history and "breeding [*race*]," Proust claims, the effects of Flaubert's style on our vision of the world should be compared to the Copernican change of perspective brought about by Kant's radical critique of pure reason:

J'ai été stupéfait, je l'avoue, de voir traité de peu doué pour écrire, un homme qui par l'usage entièrement nouveau et personnel qu'il a fait du passé défini, du passé indéfini, du participe présent, de certains pronoms et de certaines prépositions, a renouvelé presque autant notre vision des choses que Kant, avec ses Catégories, les théories de la Connaissance et de la Réalité du monde extérieur.[10]

I was, I confess, amazed to find treated as one but little gifted for literature a man who, by the entirely new and personal use that he made of the past definite, the past indefinite, the present participle, and of certain pronouns and prepositions, has renewed our vision of things almost as much as Kant, with his Categories, has renewed our theories of Knowledge and of the Reality of the external world.

Proust is stunned by Thibaudet's article. How can a writer who has so revolutionized the French language not be "un écrivain de race"? How can a writer whose grammar and syntax has so profoundly modified our vision of the world be lacking in pedigree?

Thibaudet's response to Proust's response begins with a reiteration of Proust's position in an effort to reconcile their two points of view:

> "J'ai été, dites-vous, stupéfait, je l'avoue, de voir traité de peu doué pour écrire, un homme qui ... a renouvelé presque autant notre vision des choses que Kant." J'aurais peut-être droit aussi à quelque stupéfaction devant ce rapprochement.... Mettons le style, et comme vous dites, la beauté grammaticale, à leur place, mais sachons aussi les tenir à cette place, et ne cédons pas non plus à la dangereuse mode, si commune aujourd'hui, d'introduire le nom de Kant là où il n'a que faire.[11]

> "I was," you confess, "amazed to find treated as one but little gifted for literature a man who ... has renewed our vision of things almost as much as Kant." I too am perhaps entitled to some amazement before this comparison.... Let style, and as you say, grammatical beauty have their place, but let us also know how to keep them in their place, and let us not give way to the dangerous fashion, so common today, of introducing Kant's name where it does not belong.

Let us not exaggerate, Thibaudet is telling Proust. Style and grammatical beauty have their place, a very important place, and one that should be fully acknowledged. However—and here Thibaudet must caution Proust ("mettons," "sachons," "ne cédons pas")—let us not give in to so fashionable a name as "Kant," for this kind of name-dropping has dangerous consequences for literature. Literature must not overstep its bounds; it is not philosophy: "Mettons le style, et comme vous dites, la beauté grammaticale, à leur place, mais sachons aussi les tenir à cette place." Literature must know its place; style and grammatical beauty cannot literally—let us be serious here—change our relation to the external world or the way we see things. What stuns Thibaudet in turn is not only the immodest comparison between literary style and philosophical insight but the claim that our vision of things has been utterly transformed by anything other than Flaubert's personal, i.e. psychological, experience of the world.

The disagreement between Proust and Thibaudet, it turns out, involves a question of grammar, and Thibaudet again begins by quoting Proust:

> "Cet imparfait, si nouveau dans la littérature, change entièrement l'aspect des choses et des êtres, comme font une lampe qu'on a déplacée, l'arrivée dans une maison nouvelle, [l'ancienne si elle est presque vide et qu'on est en plein déménagement]." Peut-être est-ce l'aspect des choses et des êtres, tel qu'il s'imposa à Flaubert, qui exigea l'emploi de l'imparfait, puisque l'imparfait exprime le passé dans un rapport soit avec le présent, soit avec une nature habituelle.... Ce qui fait que j'entends bien en somme ce que vous voulez dire quand vous proclamez que Flaubert a renouvelé ainsi notre vision des choses autant qu'un philosophe. Et je laisserais passer sans protestations cet ultra-bergsonisme si vous n'affirmiez que cette vision est renouvelée par un instrument non psychologique mais grammatical, non par la vision particulière de Flaubert, mais par son expression verbale. (Th 178–79)

This imperfect tense, so new to literature, entirely changes the aspect of things and beings, as do a lamp that has been moved, the arrival in a new house [or in an old one if it is almost empty and one is in the process of moving]. Perhaps it was the aspect of things and beings as they imposed themselves on Flaubert that demanded the use of the imperfect, since the imperfect tense expresses the past either in relation to the present or to a habitual state.... So I certainly do understand what you are saying when you proclaim that Flaubert has renewed our vision of things as much as any philosopher. And I might let this ultra-bergsonianism pass without protest were if not that you asserted this vision to have been renewed not by a psychological instrument but by a grammatical one, not by the particular vision of Flaubert but by his verbal expression.

Thibaudet might have let the analogy between literature and philosophy pass, he tells us, had it not been for Proust's outrageous claim about grammar. He can agree that our vision of things has been transformed ("renouvelée") by Flaubert. However—and this is the preposterous, counterintuitive claim Thibaudet feels compelled to modify—it is Flaubert's particular vision of things, it is the way in which things and beings imprinted themselves on him—and not his verbal expression—that is responsible for Flaubert's insight. Flaubert's verbal expression, "l'emploi de l'imparfait," is ordained, Thibaudet maintains, by the aspect of things and beings as they appeared to the man Flaubert.

However, in Thibaudet's conciliatory statement—"Peut-être est-ce l'aspect des choses et de êtres . . . "—following which he will concede that he can in fact understand and agree with what Proust is saying up to a point, he ends up saying exactly the opposite of what Proust is saying. "Ce qui fait," one might say, "qu['il] n'entend [r]ien" of what Proust is saying. "Peut-être est-ce l'aspect des choses et des êtres, tel qu'il s'imposa à Flaubert, qui exigea l'emploi de l'imparfait," Thibaudet conjectures. But Proust says exactly the opposite in the sentence Thibaudet has just quoted. It is perhaps not a coincidence, therefore, that Thibaudet cuts short Proust's series of metaphors at the very moment that his grammar does what it describes.[12] But even if one brackets all three metaphors, Proust's statement still seems pretty clear: "Cet imparfait, si nouveau dans la littérature, change entièrement l'aspect des choses et des êtres." And grammatically straightforward. Indeed an "analyse grammaticale" of the sentence would show that the subject of the verb ("[c]et imparfait") modifies the verb ("change"—present tense, third person singular), which is what is called in French "un verbe d'action." What this means, simply, is that the subject of the verb is the one performing the action: "this imperfect . . . changes," and not only does it change, it completely changes—"change *entièrement*." Grammatically speaking, one could not ask for a simpler predicate—following the verb, we find a "complément d'object direct," a direct object that undergoes the action of the verb. Thus "this imperfect," Flaubert's particular use of the imperfect tense, is the agent that changes—completely, utterly, "entièrement"—*the aspect of things and beings*: "Cet imparfait, si nouveau dans la littérature, change entièrement l'aspect des choses et des êtres." How is it, then, that Thibaudet turns a direct object into the subject of his sentence, reverses the direction of the action (and its emphasis) and concludes that he and Proust are in agreement: "Peut-être est-ce *l'aspect des choses et des êtres*, tel qu'il s'imposa à Flaubert, qui exigea l'emploi de l'imparfait…"?

Where "the aspect of things and beings" was for Proust the most direct of direct objects, it has become for Thibaudet not only the subject of two verbs—"s'imposa," "exigea"—but a formidable subject of coercive action. Where in Proust's description, "the aspect of things and beings" was an object that passively experienced the action of the subject, it becomes for Thibaudet a subject (and a matter) so inflexible, so rigid, so unchanging that it—"l'aspect des choses et des êtres"—imposes itself on Flaubert and commands his use of the imperfect tense. Where Proust reads Flaubert's revolutionary imperfect as changing the way we see the world, Thibaudet reads the world's unchanging aspect as imposing the imperfect on Flaubert. It is as if, in other words, Thibaudet had literally missed Flaubert's revolution by refusing to read Flaubert (and Proust) grammatically.

The paradoxical impact of reducing the grammatical to the psychological is such that Thibaudet loses the very thing that is particular to Flaubert. When, furthermore, the imperfect no longer simply refers to a past in relation to a present, when the imperfect in Flaubert absorbs and converts the contingencies of temporal difference into what Proust calls a "défilement continu, monotone, morne, indéfini" (continuous, monotonous, dreary, indeterminate procession) (Pr 315), its use functions very much like a grammar— that is, like a formal, mechanical stucture that streamlines the personal or the psychological.[13] The imperative to read grammatically, as Proust understands it, is thus an imperative to read Flaubert's grammar, but it is also the imperative to read the grammar that is Flaubert. Proust will see a machine at work in the "obsessive rhythm" of Flaubert's sentences (Pr 323); he will see a juggernaut but also "a grammatical beauty" (Pr 315). Thus to read the revolution of Flaubert is precisely to read this grammatical beauty: "il n'est pas possible à quiconque est un jour monté sur ce grand *Trottoir roulant* que sont les pages de Flaubert . . . de méconnaître qu'elles sont sans précédent dans la littérature" (it is not possible for anyone who has ever set foot on the great *moving walkway* of Flaubert's pages . . . not to realize that they are without precedent in literature) (Pr 315).

But there is yet a further implication to missing the revolution. By reducing grammar to psychology, Thibaudet loses not only grammar but also grammar's particular relation to temporality. Indeed the confusion between grammar and psychology returns as the conflation of the literal and the symbolic. Unable to read literally, Thibaudet cannot avoid missing the very thing that Proust finds most beautiful in Flaubert. "À mon avis," writes Proust, "la chose la plus belle de *L'Éducation sentimentale*, ce n'est pas une phrase, mais un blanc" (in my opinion, the most beautiful thing in the *Sentimental Education* is not a phrase but a blank) (Pr 324). This blank, at the end of Chapter 5 (Part 3), marks a pause and a chapter-break: "[E]t Frédéric, béant, reconnut Sénécal" (and Frédéric, open-mouthed, recognized Sénécal).[14] What follows, says Proust, is "un 'blanc,' un énorme 'blanc'" (Pr 324)—and without even the hint of a transition, we are thrown into the future on the very next page, not fifteen minutes into the future, but years, decades into the future:

Et Frédéric, béant, reconnut Sénécal.

Il voyagea.
Il connut la mélancholie des paquebots, les froids réveils sous la tente, l'étourdissement des paysages et des ruines, l'amertume des sympathies interrompues.
Il revint.
Il fréquenta le monde . . .
Vers la fin de l'année 1867 . . .

The raw passage of time, unencumbered by the "scoria of history," is written into an enormous "blank." The future has come and gone in the space of a blank. Hence, the surprise that we register when we begin the next chapter is the surprise of the unexpected; it is the trace left by what has already arrived and that the reader can only register as a missing.

Thibaudet will himself return to Proust's blank in his own article: "Ce que vous admirez le plus, dites-vous, dans *L'Éducation sentimentale*, c'est un blanc" (What you admire the most, as you say, in the *Sentimental Education* is a blank). However he immediately assimilates this "blank" to what he, Thibaudet, finds "most surprising" in Flaubert's literary existence, namely the blank that separates Flaubert's juvenilia from *Madame Bovary*. "Le moment le plus étonnant de l'existence littéraire de Flaubert c'est le blanc qui sépare la première *Éducation* et la première *Tentation* de *Madame Bovary*" (The most surprising moment in Flaubert's literary existence is the blank that separates the first *Éducation* and the first *Temptation* from *Madame Bovary*) (Th 174). Thibaudet has read a syntactical or grammatical marker (a blank, a form of punctuation) as a figure (a blank, a simile that refers to the development of Flaubert's literary talent). But the blank that Proust is talking about cannot simply be assumed as a figure when we read. It is first a blank, a white space on a page. And it is only because it is literally a white space on the page—*and not a figure*—that we can be shocked into consciousness, the consciousness of a future that has already taken place. One might say that figuration comes too late in this case, such that the inevitable shock that we feel when we read the opening lines of Chapter 6, awakens a feeling of pathos before the merciless automatism of time. Pathos arises, in other words, as a result of the reader's lack of preparedness for the intransigence of the "trottoir roulant."[15] Again, Thibaudet misses what is perhaps most affecting (and most personal) in the writing of Flaubert by reducing Flaubert's grammatical, syntactical innovations to the psychology of M. Flaubert.

By refusing to leave the familiar ground of human psychology, by refusing to read the Kant in Flaubert, Albert Thibaudet ends up behaving very much like those benighted thinkers in Kant's

The Conflict of the Faculties—those thinkers who fail to grasp the Copernican revolution and entangle themselves to the point of absurdity in cycles and epicycles precisely because they refuse to relinquish the standpoint from which they see the course of human things.[16] Flaubert's moving walkway, the grammatical force that is Flaubert's genius, has proved *affectively* unreadable for Thibaudet. Ironically, thus, it is from the absolute indifference and machine-like impassibility of the "trottoir roulant," from the most formal, mechanical, grammatical demolition of the personal, that there emerges in Flaubert a surprising temporality that is distinctly and uniquely "human."

Reading *Bouvard et Pécuchet*

In *Bouvard et Pécuchet*, Flaubert's last and unfinished novel, the full grammatical force of Flaubert's style enters into the novel in a way that turns out to be far more revealing of its revolutionary temporality than in any other of Flaubert's novels. For the first time, in the novel Flaubert calls his "testament," I will suggest, the monotonous, unrelenting force of the "trottoir roulant" becomes the allegorical subject of the novel: whence the absolutely unique nature of *Bouvard et Pécuchet* even in the context of Flaubert's writings.[17] Roland Barthes, who was fascinated by the novel, refers to *Bouvard et Pécuchet* as the pure essence of Flaubert.[18] In no other novel, therefore, does the imperative to read grammatically become more pressing than in *Bouvard et Pécuchet*.

The actual story of *Bouvard et Pécuchet*, like that of Barthélemy Maurice's *Les Deux Greffiers*,[19] is simple enough: two middle-aged scriveners—the one a ruddy widower, the other an irascible bachelor—meet on a park bench and strike up a friendship. An unexpected inheritance enables them to retire to the Norman countryside where, impelled by their desire to find intelligibility in the world, they study then forsake a huge number of disciplines: gardening, agriculture, arboriculture, chemistry, anatomy, physiology, astronomy, zoology, geology, archeology, history, literature, politics, magnetism, philosophy, religion, pedagogy. Four hundred pages later, discouraged and financially ruined, the two scriveners are galvanized by the same thought and begin copying once again.

However, it is hardly the story of the clerks' countless failures that makes *Bouvard et Pécuchet* "one of the most ambitious and one of the strangest books in the history of the French novel."[20] What makes the novel both unique and perplexing is rather the entry into the novel of the single-directed, force-like movement of Flaubert's grammar and syntax. However, when a grammatical movement becomes the story, the reader who continues to read (and not fall asleep—as was Flaubert's fear) cannot help but be disoriented by its strange exigency: a drive that presses onward, indefinitely, relentlessly, leveling everything in its path. As a result, *Bouvard et Pécuchet* is a book that many critics dismiss, beginning with Sartre who called it a "tentative absurde."[21] The book, as has often been remarked, leaves the reader hanging—

> Il laisse le lecteur indécis et l'esprit en suspens. Que signifie-t-il? A quoi tend-il? Qu'est-ce qu'il exalte? Qu'est-ce qu'il condamne?[22]

> It leaves the reader undecided and the mind in suspense. What does it mean? What does it strive for? What does it glorify? What does it condemn?

The reader of *Bouvard et Pécuchet* is left with nothing but questions. Nothing is certain. Roland Barthes, the great defender of *Bouvard et Pécuchet*, even declares it to be "un livre fou, au sens propre du terme" (an insane book, in the strict sense of the word).[23] The book is not addressed to the reader. Like a grammatical force, *Bouvard et Pécuchet*, is not an address at all.

It could be argued, rather, that every psychological response to *Bouvard et Pécuchet* is a symptom (and perhaps the symptom par excellence) of the grammatical force of this novel. In his vitriolic review of the book, which is exemplary not only for its violence but as always for its insight, Barbey d'Aurevilly takes this lack of address personally:

> Dans ce récit, écrasant vraiment de vulgarité et de bassesse, dans cette histoire de deux idiots qui se sont rencontrés un jour sur un banc de

promenade et se sont raccrochés par vide de tête, badauderie, flânerie, bavardage et nostalgie d'imbécilité... il n'y a pas un mot, pas un sous-entendu qui puisse faire croire que l'auteur se moque de ces deux benêts qui sont les héros de son livre, et qu'il n'est pas la dupe de ce récit prodigieux de bêtise voulue et réalisée.... Par place aussi, il est dégoûtant et odieux... car la haine du bourgeois, dans Flaubert, va jusqu'à cette fange qu'il remue en naturaliste, sans indignation, sans dégoût, sans nausée, avec l'impassibilité d'un homme qui a perdu la délicatesse de l'artiste.... –ce livre, enfin, illisible et insupportable, que l'auteur n'a pas fini et, qui sait? peut-être arrêté et étranglé par l'ennui qu'il se causait à lui-même, et que le lecteur ne finira pas, à coup sûr, plus que lui, mais finira certainement bien avant d'être arrivé, comme lui, au chiffre affreux de *quatre cents* pages!....[24]

In this narrative, which is truly overwhelming in its vulgarity and its baseness, in this story about two idiots who happen to meet one day on a park bench and who come together in their vacuousness, their idle curiosity, their loafing, chatter and imbecilic nostalgia... there is not one word, not one inference that might make us believe that the author is mocking the two ninnies who are the heroes of his book, and that he is not himself dupe of a narrative so prodigious in its stupidity, a stupidity both desired and realized.... In places, it is also disgusting and odious... for Flaubert's hatred of the bourgeois drags us into the muck, which, given his naturalist tendencies, he stirs up without indignation, without disgust, without nausea, with the impassibility of a man who has lost the refinement of the artist.... –in the end, this unreadable, intolerable book that the author did not finish and, who knows? perhaps, blocked and strangled by the boredom he was causing himself, a book that the reader will definitely not finish either, but will certainly put down well before the ghastly count of *four hundred* pages!...

Barbey d'Aurevilly responds to Flaubert's indifference as if to a personal affront. The histrionics and fury unleashed in his review are those of a man who is so beside himself that he must appeal, in his defense, to a tragedy—for Flaubert was literally struck down, in the middle of writing Chapter 10, by an apoplectic stroke, which left him dying on his sofa: "et qui sait? peut-être arrêté et étranglé par l'ennui qu'il se causait lui-même..." Four hundred pages, says Barbey d'Aurevilly, in which there is not a word, not an inference—"pas

un mot, pas un sous-entendu"—that might give the reader an indication as to how to read the novel. The reader has no idea, and above
all no textual proof whatsoever, as to whether the author is making fun of his two "bonshommes" or even that he thinks unkindly
of them. The reader cannot know, cannot decide conclusively—
anything, were it the status of "la bêtise" (the stupidity) that "consists in wanting to conclude."[25] The reader cannot know for sure
whether Flaubert is in fact chiding the methods and aspirations of
Bouvard and Pécuchet. Yet, Barbey d'Aurevilly decides. Or rather,
he reacts to an intolerable impassivity by giving it a voice. Barbey
d'Aurevilly is responding to a grammatical force, psychologically.
One might say that he gives it the voice of his own ambivalence.[26]

Moreover, this psychological trap into which readers and critics of
Bouvard et Pécuchet seem so readily to fall, is set by Flaubert himself.
Flaubert's letters document an ever-increasing indignation before
"la bêtise et l'injustice" (the stupidity and injustice) of his time (GS
139). From his letters, it would seem that Flaubert had waited his
entire life to disgorge his indignation on his contemporaries. And
nowhere is this explosive finish more overdetermined than in the
letters that describe the project of *Bouvard et Pécuchet*:

[J]e médite une chose où *j'exhalerai ma colère*. Oui, je me débarrasserai,
enfin, de ce qui m'étouffe. Je vomirai sur mes contemporains le dégoût
qu'ils m'inspirent. Dussé-je m'en casser la poitrine, ce sera large et
violent. (CB 4: 583–84)

J'étudie l'histoire des théories médicales et des traités d'éducation.
Après quoi je passerai à d'autres lectures. J'avale force volumes et je
prends des notes. . . . Tout cela dans l'unique but de cracher sur mes
contemporains le dégoût qu'ils m'inspirent. Je vais enfin leur dire
ma manière de penser, exhaler mon ressentiment, vomir ma haine,
expectorer mon fiel, éjaculer ma colère, déterger mon indignation.
(CB 4: 582–83)

[I] am contemplating something in which *I will vent my rage*. Yes,
I will finally get rid of what chokes me. I shall vomit on my
contemporaries the disgust they inspire in me. Were I to burst my
chest while doing it, it will be broad and violent.

I am studying the history of medical theories and treatises on education. After which, I will move on to other things. I am ingesting volume upon volume and I take notes.... All of this with the sole aim of discharging on my contemporaries the disgust that they inspire in me. I will finally tell them my way of thinking, vent my resentment, vomit my hatred, expectorate my bile, ejaculate my rage, deterge my indignation.

Reading these letters, one cannot help but expect *Bouvard et Pécuchet* to be the venting of a lifetime, "le livre des vengences," an excremental eruption of Gargantuan proportion. And yet, and yet—*Bouvard et Pécuchet* is Flaubert's most comic, most controlled and enigmatic production. The only explosion in the text is the one that occurs on the last page of Chapter 2 and whose explanation is immediately given:

> Tout à coup, avec un bruit d'obus, l'alambic éclata en vingt morceaux, qui bondirent jusqu'au plafond, crevant les marmites, aplatissant les écumoires, fracassant les verres; le charbon s'éparpilla, le fourneau fut démoli—et le lendemain, Germaine retrouva une spatule dans la cour.
>
> La force de la vapeur avait rompu l'instrument, d'autant que la cucurbite se trouvait boulonnée au chapiteau. (BP 115)

> Suddenly, with the detonation of a shell, the still burst into a score of pieces which leapt to the ceiling, cracking the pots, knocking over the ladles, shattering the glasses; the coals were scattered, the furnace demolished—and the next day Germaine picked up a spatula in the yard.
>
> The pressure of the steam had broken the apparatus—naturally so, as the cucurbit turned out to be blocked at the mouth. (BP 73)

This mini, humorous, textual explosion is a terrible disappointment in the face of the apocalyptic promise of Flaubert's letters. As Barbey d'Aurevilly himself concedes, there is not a word that can be traced back to the man of letters. And Barbey d'Aurevilly is quite specific in his indictment: "la haine du bourgeois, dans Flaubert, va jusqu'à cette fange qu'il remue en naturaliste, *sans indignation, sans dégoût, sans nausée.*" Flaubert, says d'Aurevilly, has entirely disappeared into the incredible "platitude" of his novel in which one finds only tasteless descriptions of shameful things. In other words, there is no perceptible indignation, no discernible disgust, no apparent nausea in this novel at all. And this, in the last analysis, this flat lining of affect, this absence of horizon, is what proves so unreadable to Barbey d'Aurevilly. Like *Candide*, the explosive force of *Bouvard et Pécuchet*—"la griffe du lion" (the claw of the lion)—is wholly inseparable from "cette conclusion tranquille, bête comme la vie" (the peaceful conclusion, as stupid as life) (CB 2: 78).[27] To read the explosive force of Flaubert's "trottoir roulant," to read the "human" dimension of this movement, therefore, one must begin by reading grammatically.

Reading Bouvard and Pécuchet Reading

In none of Flaubert's novels is the imperative to read grammatically more pressing, thus, than in *Bouvard et Pécuchet*. If the movement of the "trottoir roulant" can and should be read as a force of grammar, then the novel that tells its story can provide nothing in the way of explanation. Like grammar, in other words, the movement of the "trottoir roulant" moves from sameness to sameness according to a system whose underlying principle is totalization.

But can a movement whose formalism is its force be anything but empty? From the time of the publication of *Bouvard et Pécuchet*, critics have maintained that Bouvard and Pécuchet's encyclopedic quest comes full circle (or full spiral) in the end. As Flaubert's final notes for the volume indicate, Bouvard and Pécuchet were to take up copying once again in the conclusion—

> Bonne idée nourrie en secret par chacun d'eux. Ils se la dissimulent – De temps à autre, ils sourient, quand elle leur vient; —puis se la communiquent simultanément: copier. (BP 414)

> A good idea cherished secretly by each of them. They hide it from one another – From time to time they smile when it occurs to them;—then at last communicate it simultaneously to each other: to copy. (BP 347–48)

In this regard, the subsequent addition of "comme autrefois [*as before*]" by Caroline Commanville seems convincingly to render the dialectical movement of the quest. In fact, many editions of *Bouvard et Pécuchet* unwittingly reproduced her apocryphal locution. Must it be conceded, then, that the narrative follows a purely dialectical logic whereby its unfolding tells us only what was always already there from the start? What came first: Bouvard and Pécuchet's Copy[28] or *Bouvard et Pécuchet*?

On the one hand, therefore, it would seem that *Bouvard et Pécuchet* tells a story in which the innumerable failures of Bouvard and Pécuchet are endlessly recuperated by the grammatical force of the imperfect, a force that operates like a dialectic. On the other hand, however, I will suggest that the very movement from sameness to sameness, from imperfect to imperfect, not only repeats the sameness of the past—*it also projects this sameness into the future*. What if, furthermore, this shift in the temporality of "sameness"— precisely because it was a matter of grammatical indifference—were something irreducible to a force of indifferentiation?

TIME AS TELEOLOGY

On the one hand, thus, and for much of the novel, Bouvard and Pécuchet's course of study follows an explicitly dialectical sequence. Gardening, agriculture, arboriculture, canning, distillation, chemistry, anatomy, physiology, astronomy, zoology, geology, archeology, history, literature, politics, magnetism, philosophy, religion, pedagogy: one project leads to the next, and although every project ends in failure, every failure points to a new discipline, and every discipline promises to fill the crucial gap in Bouvard and Pécuchet's education. Failure, in this context, is the determinate negation that sustains the quest. The explosion of the still, which puts an end to Bouvard and Pécuchet's confectionery dream-cream ("la Bouvarine") in Chapter 2, immediately prompts their study of science. If only they had known the basic principles of chemistry, such an accident would not have occurred. The study of science will prove unsatisfactory, as will the study of history, as will the study of literature, etc. However, each newly discovered lacuna further stimulates Bouvard and Pécuchet in their totalizing quest.

The dialectical nature of failure emerges in the simple past (passé simple). Hence, the simple past is the tense that stands witness to each of Bouvard and Pécuchet's countless activities. From their very first day in Chavignolles, the simple past becomes the simplest expression of their hopes and aspirations: "Bouvard planta une pivoine au milieu du gazon.... Pécuchet fit creuser devant la cuisine, un large trou" (Bouvard planted a peony in the middle of the lawn.... Pécuchet had a large pit dug in front of the kitchen) (BP 77; 39–40). The simple past expects and promises the new, whether in the garden (Pécuchet)—"Il sema les graines de plusieurs variétés dans des assiettes remplies de terreau.... Il fit toutes les tailles suivant les préceptes du bon jardinier, respecta les fleurs, laissa se nouer les fruits, en choisit un sur chaque bras, supprima les autres..." (He sowed several different kinds of seeds in pans with mould.... He made all his cuttings according to the instructions of the gardening manual, left the flowers intact, allowed the fruit to form a cluster, chose one on each stem, picked off the others) (BP 86; 47)—or in the fields (Bouvard):

> Excité par Pécuchet, il eut le délire de l'engrais. Dans la fosse aux composts furent entassés des branchages, du sang, des boyaux, des plumes.... Il employa la liqueur belge, le lizier suisse, la lessive *Da-Olmi*, des harengs saurs, du varech, des chiffons, fit venir du guano, tâcha d'en fabriquer—et poussant jusqu'au bout ses principes... il supprima les lieux d'aisances. (BP 89)

> Egged on by Pécuchet, he had a frenzy for manure. In the compost-trench were flung together boughs, blood, entrails, feathers.... He employed Belgian dressing, Swiss fertilizer, lye, pickled herrings, seaweed, rags; he sent for guano, and tried to manufacture it; then, pushing his tenets to the extreme.... He suppressed the privies. (BP 50)

But direct action, as Bouvard soon discovers, is a double-edged sword: "Le colza fut chétif, l'avoine médiocre; et le blé vendit fort mal, à cause de son odeur" (The colza was meager, the oats poor; and the wheat sold badly because of its smell) (BP 89; 50). Where at first the assertiveness of the simple past expressed positive possibility, it quickly comes to signal a call to arms: "Bouvard tâcha de conduire les abricotiers. Ils se révoltèrent. Il abattit leurs troncs à ras du sol; aucun ne repoussa" (Bouvard tried to train the apricot trees. They rebelled. He forced their stems down to the level of the soil; none of them grew up again) (BP 96; 56). A battle with nature in the simple past proves an unwinnable fight.

And the simple past does not even represent nature's preferred tense. As if to add insult to injury, the imperfect returns, like a force of nature, laying low what remains of Bouvard and Pécuchet's achievements in the simple past:

> Toutes les meules, çà et là, flambaient...—au milieu de la plaine dénudée, dans le calme du soir. (BP 92)

> Sous les flammes dévorantes la paille se tordait avec des crépitations, les grains de blé vous cinglaient la figure comme des grains de plomb. Puis, la meule s'écroulait par terre en un large brasier, d'où s'envolaient des étincelles; —et des moires ondulaient sur cette masse rouge, qui offrait dans les alternances de sa couleur, des parties roses comme du vermillon, et d'autres brunes comme du sang caillé. La nuit était venue; le vent soufflait; des tourbillons de fumé enveloppaient la foule; —une flammèche, de temps à autre, passait sur le ciel noir. (BP 92–93)

> All the ricks, dotted here and there in the middle of the bare plain, were blazing like volcanoes in the evening stillness. (BP 52)

> In the devouring flames the straw twisted and crackled, grains of wheat peppered their faces like lead pellets. Then the stack fell to the ground, a great brazier, sending sparks flying up. The red mass undulated with a sheen like watered silk, which showed in its changing lines parts that were vermilion red and others brown like clotted blood. Night had fallen, the wind was blowing; wisps of smoke enveloped the crowd. Sputters of flame, from time to time, passed across the black sky. (BP 53)

The imperfect tense emerges as a sheer and simple (even beautiful) force, an absolutely disinterested force of nature. Beyond the battle scenes of the passé simple and the phantasmatic projections of indirect discourse in what may be Flaubert's most abstract use of the "discours indirect libre"—"Le vent s'amusait à jeter bas les rames des haricots" (The wind threw down the bean props in its sport) (BP 85; 47)—the eternal imperfect returns.

In the wake of this natural catastrophe, however, Bouvard and Pécuchet will not only search for the cause of the fire, they will actively disavow the possibility of spontaneous combustion: "et au lieu de reconnaître avec tout le monde que la paille humide s'était enflammée spontanément, ils soupçonnèrent une vengeance" (instead of recognizing, like everybody else, that the damp straw had flamed up of itself spontaneously, they suspected a revenge) (BP 94; 54). The notion of a spontaneous combustion is rejected by Bouvard and Pécuchet, precisely, it would seem, because its possibility cannot be conceived of in simple oppositional terms. In fact, for most of the novel Bouvard and Pécuchet will hold fast to the promise of dialectical progress.

REVOLUTION

It is interesting to note, however, that at the heart of the novel lies an example of an event whose very subsumption by the forces of order leaves an indelible mark on Bouvard and Pécuchet. It is Flaubert's great irony, I will suggest, to have placed a truly irreversible event—the trauma of Bouvard and Pécuchet—in the middle of the farcical, historical reversal whose dates punctuate Chapter 6. Chapter 6 will begin and end with a date: "Dans la matinée du 25 février, on apprit à Chavignolles, par un individu venant de Falaise, que Paris était couvert de barricades—et le lendemain, la proclamation de la République fut affichée sur la mairie" (On the morning of 25th February 1848 the news was brought to Chavignolles, by a wayfarer from Falaise, that Paris was under barricades—and the next day the proclamation of the Republic was posted up outside the town hall) (BP 226; 173); "C'était le 3 décembre 1851" (It was the 3rd of December 1851) (BP 257; 201). It ends with the terrible massacre that takes place on the boulevard des Capucines in the days following Louis-Napoléon Bonaparte's coup d'État of December 1851: in other words, it ends in exactly the same spot (literally) as the shooting that touched off the 1848 revolution with which the chapter begins.

Bouvard and Pécuchet alone note the reversals that are taking place around them. The freedom tree, Bouvard and Pécuchet's gift to Chavignolles, planted and blessed by the curé at the beginning of Chapter 6, is cut down squarely in the middle of the chapter with Bouvard as its only witness:

> Les arbres de la liberté furent abattus généralement. Chavignolles obéit à la consigne. Bouvard vit de ses yeux les morceaux de son peuplier sur une brouette. Ils servirent à chauffer les gendarmes; —et on offrit la souche à M. le Curé—qui l'avait béni, pourtant! quelle derision! (BP 244)

> The trees of liberty were everywhere pulled down. Chavignolles obeyed the order. With his own eyes, Bouvard saw bits of his poplar on a wheelbarrow. They helped to keep the policemen warm—and the stump was offered to M. le Curé, who had blessed it! What irony! (BP 189)

With his own eyes, Bouvard sees the symbol of the republic torn down and turned over to the new party of law and order. By the end of the chapter, it is as if the revolution had never occurred, as if it had literally been reduced to a "fiction." Finally, when the 1851 massacre meets with the general approval of Chavignolles, Bouvard will throw up his hands in disgust: "Tout me dégoûte. Vendons . . . notre baraque—et allons au tonnerre de Dieu, chez les sauvages!" (I'm sick of everything. Let's sell this shanty—and go to the sound of God's thunder, among the savages!) (BP 258; 203). What is irreversible, revolutionary, on the other hand, occurs without passing onto any world-historical stage.

Bouvard and Pécuchet cannot forget Chavignolles's violent erasure of 1848. For them, there can be no return to pre-revolutionary times. The truly revolutionary event is thus not what takes place on the boulevard des Capucines but what occurs as a shift in Bouvard and Pécuchet's encyclopedic quest, a shift whose symptom becomes an analytic—indeed a critical-linguistic—power in the face of injustice. In the case of Gorgu who has been arrested for sedition, Marescot claims they are defending a dangerous man:

> —"Vraiment" dit Bouvard, "pour quelques paroles!..."
> —"Quand la parole amène des crimes, cher monsieur, permettez!"
> —"Cependant" reprit Pécuchet, "quelle démarcation établir entre les phrases innocentes et les coupables? Telle chose défendue maintenant sera par la suite applaudie." Et il blâma la manière féroce dont on traitait les insurgés.
> Marescot allégua naturellement la defense de la Société, le Salut Public, loi suprême. (BP 241)

> "Really," said Bouvard, "for a few words!..."
> "But words lead to crimes, my dear sir, I assure you!"
> "And yet," said Pécuchet, "how can we draw a line between the innocence and guilt of a phrase? Something that's forbidden now will be commended later on," and he censured the harshness with which the insurgents were being treated.
> Marescot naturally advanced the protection of society, the public safety, the highest law. (BP 187)

For Marescot, public safety speaks for itself; it is the highest law and that which commands all the rest. But it is not he who introduces the term "naturally" here. "Naturally" emanates, rather, from Bouvard and Pécuchet's utter disillusionment with the language of politics, for they expect Marescot to respond exactly as he does. With "naturally," Bouvard and Pécuchet are indicting the legacy— the murderous legacy—of allegations made in the name of "public safety": "Sa doctrine du salut public les avait indignés. Les conservateurs parlaient maintenant comme Robespierre" (His doctrine of public safety had made them indignant. The conservatives were now talking like Robespierre) (BP 241–42; 187). For the first time in their encyclopedic quest, Bouvard and Pécuchet have encountered a radical negativity, indeed a language of power that resists all dialectical assimilation. For the first time, in other words, the very possibility of progress, on which their quest is predicated, has been shaken in its foundation. They have encountered something heterogeneous to the space of knowledge.

PRESENT DISRUPTIONS: THE INTEMPORAL PRESENT

In the midst of their dialectical travails, Bouvard and Pécuchet are further confronted by a tense that squares neither with the activity of the "passé simple" nor with monotony of the "imparfait." This tense, the "intemporal present"[29] of truth and objectivity, is the sign of a specifically textual encounter. From the very beginning, Bouvard and Pécuchet's encyclopedic quest has revolved around the study and absorption of books. Not only must they get hold of the right books for every new project (have them sent to them, choose the best ones, the ones that will dispense with all the others),[30] they must struggle to make sense of these books. For the "intemporal present" makes possible the coexistence of irreconcilable "truths." The more books they read, the more Bouvard and Pécuchet grow confused by differing—if not blatantly contradictory—factual accounts:

> Ainsi, pour la marne, Puvis la recommande; le manuel Roret la combat.
> Quant au plâtre, malgré l'exemple de Franklin, Rieffel et M. Rigaud n'en paraissent pas enthousiasmés.
> Les jachères, selon Bouvard, étaient un préjugé gothique. Cependant, Leclerc note les cas où elles sont presque indispensables. Gasparin cite un lyonnais qui pendant un demi-siècle a cultivé des céréales sur le même champ; cela renverse la théorie des assolements. Tull exalte les labours au préjudice des engrais; et voilà le major Betson qui supprime les engrais, avec les labours! (BP 88)

> Thus, as regards marl, Puvis recommends it; Roret's manual opposes it.
> As to plaster, despite Franklin's example, Rieffel and M. Rigaud do not seem enthusiastic.
> Fallows, according to Bouvard, were a Gothic prejudice. Yet Leclerc notes cases where they are almost indispensable. Gasparin quotes a Lyonnais farmer who, for half a century, cultivated cereals in the same field; that upsets the theory of crop rotations. Tull exalts ploughing to the detriment of manure; and here is Major Betson who abolishes manure for ploughing! (BP 49)

Bouvard and Pécuchet not only confuse themselves. Their muddle is communicated in the text, by the text; it is passed on to the reader. The intemporal present blurs the lines of enunciation such that it becomes impossible for the reader to determine who is speaking at any given moment. As Pécuchet later exclaims in exasperation: "Where is the rule, then . . . ?" (BP 99; 59). Are Bouvard and Pécuchet discussing alternative farming methods? Is this an exchange between them? Is it Bouvard who cites Puvis? Or is it Pécuchet? And is it the same speaker who refutes Puvis with Roret or the other speaker? But who is "the other"? Who was "the same"? In Flaubert's use of indirect discourse, here—if it is indirect discourse—nothing is certain. Bouvard is the one who mentions "fallows," but can he also be the one to cite Leclerc and refute his own "prejudice"? And who concludes that the theory of crop rotations has been disproved? Is it Bouvard? Or Pécuchet? Or is it Gasparin who cites the Lyonnais farmer in order to prove just this point? Or is it Bouvard (Pécuchet?) who recalls Gasparin's reference to the Lyonnais farmer in order to infer from it support for Bouvard's initial "prejudice"? Or is it the nameless Lyonnais farmer who is being paraphrased here and whose farming practices clearly disprove "the theory of crop rotations"? How indirect is the discourse, in other words? Is it once, twice, or thrice removed from the reader? How present is this intemporal present? We cannot know, just as Bouvard and Pécuchet do not know whether to plow or fertilize their fields.

Moreover, the intemporal present soon threatens the very foundations upon which scientific truth was to be established:

Jusqu'alors ils avaient cru à l'insalubrité des endroits humides. Pas du tout! Casper les déclare moins mortels que les autres. On ne se baigne pas dans la mer sans avoir rafraîchi sa peau. Béguin veut qu'on s'y jette en pleine transpiration. Le vin pur après la soupe passe pour excellent à l'estomac. Lévy l'accuse d'altérer les dents. . . .

Qu'est-ce donc que l'hygiène?

—"Vérité en deçà des Pyrénées, erreur au delà" affirme M. Lévy; et Becquerel ajoute qu'elle n'est pas une science. (BP 136)

Until then they had believed that damp places were unhealthy. Not at all! Casper declares them less fatal than others. One cannot bathe in

the sea without refreshing the skin. Béguin would have one dive into it while profusely sweating. Unwatered wine, after soup, is passed as admirable for the stomach. Lévy accuses it of harming the teeth....
What then is hygiene?
"Truth on one side of the Pyrenees, falsehood on the other," affirms M. Lévy; and Becquerel adds that it is not a science. (BP 91–92)

If the same things can be both healthy and unhealthy at the same time, then hygiene can have no scientific value. The cultural irony, set forth by M. Lévy, absolutely confirms Bouvard and Pécuchet's thinking about hygiene. But how is it that we have we gotten from "damp places" to salt water? Who has made this transition (and therefore this argument) possible? Is it Casper who merely asserts that "damp places" are less dangerous—less "fatal [*mortels*]"—than other places? Is it Béguin who has something to say about the virtues of salt water? Or is it Bouvard and Pécuchet who make the transition between dampness and total immersion, between Casper and Béguin? Because the passage from "damp places" (Casper) to salt water (Béguin) escapes all personal assignation, it seems to have posed a problem for one English translator of *Bouvard and Pécuchet*, whose chosen translation brings out the impassability of this passage. The translator does this by changing the meaning of the transitional phrase:

> Up till then they had believed that damp places are unhealthy. Not at all! Casper asserts that they are less dangerous than others. *One should not bathe in the sea without first cooling down one's skin* [On ne se baigne pas dans la mer sans avoir rafraîchi sa peau]. Béguin thinks it better to plunge in actually sweating [my emphasis].[31]

Instead of positive refreshment (one cannot not be refreshed...), we have an actual, negative prescription (do not bathe in the sea without first cooling down...). Can we or can we not bathe without being refreshed? Like Bouvard and Pécuchet, we are left hanging at the end of this paragraph, without any consensus about the hygiene of saltwater bathing. In other words, the intemporal present leads to a dilemma that is not resolved but rather taken up by the dialectic. Although Bouvard and Pécuchet have moved on to astronomy within a page, the intemporal present has introduced the notion of a moment or space of impossible passage.

PRESENT DISRUPTIONS: THE TESTIMONIAL PRESENT

Although Bouvard and Pécuchet will spend the post-revolutionary chapters in search of a bottom line with which they might rest secure in their knowledge, a terrible desperation has taken hold of their quest. Nothing, it would seem—not love, or gymnastics, or magnetism, or spiritism, or philosophy, or religion—can quite reverse the trend. Their depression comes in waves of verbs in the imperfect tense:

> Des jours tristes commencèrent.
>
> Ils n'étudiaient plus dans la peur de déceptions; les habitants de Chavignolles s'écartaient d'eux; les journaux tolérés n'apprenaient rien—et leur solitude était profonde, leur désœuvrement complet.
>
> Quelquefois, ils ouvraient un livre, et le refermaient; à quoi bon? En d'autres jours, ils avaient l'idée de nettoyer le jardin, au bout d'un quart d'heure une fatigue les prenait; ou de voir leur ferme, ils en revenaient écœurés; ou de s'occuper de leur ménage, Germaine poussait des lamentations; ils y renoncèrent. (BP 260)

> Gloomy days began.
>
> They no longer pursued their studies, for fear of disillusionment; the people of Chavignolles cold-shouldered them, the privileged newspapers gave them no information, and their solitude was unbroken, their idleness complete.
>
> Sometimes they opened a book, only to close it again—what was the use? On other days they resolved to tidy the garden, but at the end of a quarter of an hour they would be worn out; or to go and inspect their farm, but they came back disheartened; or to give an eye to the housekeeping, which set Germaine protesting, and they abandoned the idea. (BP 204)

Their occupations of the past no longer sustain them. The happy days, their age of innocence seem so distant from them now:

> Pourquoi ne suivaient-ils plus les moissonneurs? Où étaient les jours qu'ils entraient dans les fermes cherchant partout des antiquités? Rien maintenant n'occasionnerait ces heures si douces qu'emplissaient la

distillerie ou la Littérature. Un abîme les en séparait. Quelque chose d'irrévocable était venu. (BP 320–21)

Why did they no longer follow the harvesters? Where were the days when they went into farms, looking for antiques? Nothing, now, brought those delightful hours that distilling or literature had filled. They were separated from them by an abyss. Something irrevocable had occurred. (BP 259)

Something irreversible has occurred. And yet, syntactically, nothing but a lone and mawkish conditional separates the imperfect of the past ("suivaient," "entraient," "emplissaient") from the imperfect of the present ("séparait," "était [venu]"). There remains only the future, but soon the future, it too, will meet with a similar fate. In search of an antidote to their depression, Bouvard and Pécuchet resolve to "take a walk in the fields as they used to" (BP 260). What they meet with, however, is not simply nature's sumptuous display of verbs in the imperfect tense:

—De petits nuages moutonnaient dans le ciel, le vent balançait les clochettes des avoines, le long d'un pré un ruisseau murmurait, quand tout à coup une odeur infecte les arrêta; et ils virent sur des cailloux, entre des joncs, la charogne d'un chien.
    Les quatres membres étaient désséchés. Le rictus de la gueule découvrait sous des babines bleuâtres des crocs d'ivoire; à la place du ventre, c'était un amas de couleur terreuse, et qui semblait palpiter tant grouillait dessus la vermine. Elle s'agitait, frappée par le soleil, sous le bourdonnement des mouches, dans cette intolérable odeur, une odeur féroce et comme dévorante. (BP 321)

—Little clouds were like wool in the sky, the wind swayed the heads of oats, a brook murmured by a meadow, when suddenly a horrible smell stopped them, and they saw, on the stones between the briers, the corpse of a dog.
    The four legs were dried up. The grinning jaw revealed ivory fangs beneath blue chops; instead of the belly there was an earth-colored mass that seemed to palpitate, so thickly did it pullulate with vermin. It stirred, beaten by the sun, under the buzzing of flies, in that intolerable stench—a fierce, and as it were, devouring odor. (BP 260)

Bouvard and Pécuchet encounter the future—their future: "Nous serons un jour comme ça" ("One day we shall be like that") (BP 321; 260)—grinning, as it were, in the imperfect. Past, present, and future: time as such has fallen prey to the all-consuming force of the imperfect. Not only can all of life be represented by the imperfect, life itself has become identified with its intolerable movement to which only death promises to put an end—

> Ils tâchaient de l'imaginer [la mort] sous la forme d'une nuit intense, d'un trou sans fond, d'un évanouissement continu. N'importe quoi valait mieux que cette existence monotone, absurde, et sans espoir. (BP 321)

> They tried to imagine death in the form of a very dark night, a bottomless pit, a never-ending swoon. Anything at all was better than this monotonous, absurd and hopeless existence. (BP 260)

Having examined the question of suicide, Bouvard and Pécuchet briefly deliberate on the best method of death. They decide to hang themselves. Their suicide will of course fail like every other project in this novel. What disrupts this particular project, however, takes a familiar and ironic form:

> La chandelle était par terre—et Pécuchet debout sur une des chaises avec le câble dans sa main.
>   L'esprit d'imitation emporta Bouvard: —"Attends-moi!" Et il montait sur l'autre chaise quand s'arrêtant tout à coup:
>   —"Mais... nous n'avons pas fait notre testament?"
>   —"Tiens! c'est juste!" (BP 323–24)

> The candle was on the floor, and Pécuchet standing on one of the chairs, with the rope in his hand.
>   A mimetic desire took hold of Bouvard: "Wait for me!" And he was climbing on the other chair, when suddenly stopping:
>   "But... we've not made our wills."
>   "My word! That's true." (BP 262)

Bouvard and Pécuchet cannot die intestate. They have forgotten to write their wills. For the second time, in other words, there occurs in Flaubert's text a testamentary disruption whose (untimely) time-liness will drive life forward. Once again, the arrival of salvation in testamentary form occurs in response to the inexorable movement of (life in) the "imparfait."

Similarly, in the Prologue,[32] at a moment when the hopeless monotony of the imperfect threatens to overwhelm them, Bouvard and Pécuchet are saved by an untimely missive:

> La monotonie du bureau leur devenait odieuse. Continuellement le grattoir et la sandaraque, le même encrier, les mêmes plumes et les mêmes compagnons! Les jugeant stupides, ils leur parlaient de moins en moins.... Autrefois, ils se trouvaient presque heureux. Mais leur métier les humiliait depuis qu'ils s'estimaient davantage; —et ils se renforçaient dans ce dégoût, s'exaltaient mutuellement, se gâtaient....
>
> Quelle situation abominable! Et nul moyen d'en sortir! Pas même d'espérance!
>
> Un après-midi (c'était le 20 janvier 1839) Bouvard étant à son comptoir reçut une lettre, apportée par le facteur. (BP 62)

> The monotony of the office became odious. Always the scratching penknife and the sand-sprinkler, the same inkwell, the same pens, and the same companions! Judging the latter stupid, they spoke to them less and less.... At one time they had been almost happy; but now that they had a higher opinion of themselves, their work humiliated them;—and they made common cause in this disgust, exciting and spoiling one another....
>
> It was an abominable situation. And no way out! Not even a hope! One afternoon (it was the twentieth of January 1839), when Bouvard was at his desk, a letter was brought by the postman. (BP 27)

The letter, we learn, is an official letter from a notary informing Bouvard of his inheritance. The shock is twofold, for not only does salvation come so unexpectedly—"Bouvard étant à son comptoir reçut une lettre"—but it comes in the form of a present tense that asserts a truth wholly incompatible with the past. "Je vous prie," reads the letter, "de vous rendre en mon étude, pour y prendre connaissance du testament de votre père naturel.... Ce testament contient en votre faveur une disposition très importante" (I request your presence at my office to become acquainted with the will of your natural father.... This will contains an important bequest in your favor) (BP 63; 28). In this legal summons, Bouvard comes into his inheritance by discovering his identity. The shock of this present, which transforms an uncle into a father, suddenly opens the future to new possibility.

The legacy of Bouvard's father returns again in the very scene that precedes Bouvard and Pécuchet failed suicide attempt:

> Et chacun tirant à soi la boîte, le plateau tomba; une des tasses fut brisée, la dernière du beau service en porcelaine.
> Bouvard pâlit. —"Continue! saccage! ne te gêne pas!"
> —"Grand malheur, vraiment!"
> —"Oui! un malheur! Je la tenais de mon père!"
> —"Naturel" ajouta Pécuchet, en ricanant.
> —"Ah! tu m'insultes!" (BP 323)

> And, each pulling the caddy towards himself, the tray fell; one of the cups was broken, the last of their beautiful china service.
> Bouvard turned pale. –"Go on! wreck everything! don't hold back! "A great misfortune, indeed!"
> "Yes! A misfortune! It was from my father."
> "Your natural father," added Pécuchet, sniggering.
> "Ah! now you're insulting me!" (BP 262)

The spirit of Bouvard's father returns in a broken teacup. And it is perhaps this spirit that calls (by association or metonymy) for a testament at this point of no return. What returns in Bouvard and Pécuchet's botched suicide is thus not only the intolerable monotony of the imperfect tense but also, simultaneously, the driving force or life drive of what is called a "testament."

Futurity

Tourgueneff me sermonne pour que je reprenne au plus vite mon grand bouquin sur mes deux Cloportes. Il en est toqué. Mais les difficultés d'un pareil livre m'épouvantent. Et pourtant je ne voudrais pas mourir, avant de l'avoir fait. Car en définitive, c'est mon *testament*. (GS 524, my emphasis)[33]

In the final pages of the novel—or in what would have been its transition to Bouvard and Pécuchet's Copy had Flaubert lived to write it—we find the traces of a shift from one notion of time to another. The move from time as teleology (Bouvard and Pécuchet's encyclopedic quest) to time as tautology (Bouvard and Pécuchet's Copy) was to have absorbed time itself into the endless stutter of the walkway and to have marked the final languishing of difference. Like a thermodynamic force,[34] the Copy of Bouvard and Pécuchet would have "absorb[ed] all sorts of texts, and cruelly level[led] out the most heterogeneous of references, the most disparate of 'authors'."[35] In the last known scenario for the end of the novel, it is understood that Bouvard and Pécuchet will copy everything: "Ils copièrent... tout ce qui leur tomba sous la main... longue énumération... les notes des auteurs précédemment lus,—vieux papiers achetés au poids à la manufacture de papier voisine" (They copied... everything that came into their hands... long enumerations... notes on authors already read,—old papers bought by the pound from the nearby paper factory) (BP 442). Or, as Flaubert writes in an earlier scenario: "Ils copient au hasard... cornets de tabac, vieux journaux, lettres perdues, affiches" (They copy haphazardly... tobacco pouches, old newspapers, lost letters, posters) (BP 442). They copy everything without exception: "Parallèles: crimes des peuples—des rois—bienfaits de la religion, crimes de la religion" (Parallels: the crimes of the people—of kings—the blessings of religion, the crimes of religion) (BP 442). And one day—in what would have been Chapter 12—"XII = conclusion" according to Flaubert (BP 443)—they come across a copy of an official letter from Vaucorbeil, the doctor of Chavignolles, to the Préfet:

Le Préfet lui avait demandé si Bouvard et Pécuchet n'étaient pas des fous dangereux. La lettre du docteur est un rapport confidentiel expliquant que ce sont deux imbéciles inoffensifs....

—"Qu'allons-nous en faire?" —Pas de réflexion! copions! Il faut
que la page s'emplisse, que le "monument" se complète. –égalité de
tout, du bien et du mal, du Beau et du laid, de l'insignifiant et du
caractéristique. Il n'y a de vrai que les phénomènes.—

Finir sur la vue des deux bonshommes penchés sur leur pupitre, et
copiant. (BP 443)

The Préfet had inquired as to whether Bouvard and Pécuchet were
not in fact dangerous madmen. The doctor's letter is a confidential
report explaining that they are two harmless imbeciles.

—"What shall we do?" —One should not reflect! let us copy! The
page must be filled, let the "monument" complete itself. —equality of
everything, good and evil, the Beautiful and the ugly, the insignificant
and the characteristic. The only truth is phenomena.—

End with the image of the two men hunched over their desks,
copying.

But a question will always remain: would Bouvard and Pécuchet—
precisely by leveling out all textual accounts in their Copy ("cornets de tabac, vieux journaux, lettres perdues, affiches")—not have
become, in some sense, the best, most faithful readers of Flaubert?
Would their Copy not have taken Flaubert's style to its most literal
(and perhaps modern) extreme by linking heterogeneous things,
by stringing discontinuous things together, and thereby arriving at
a terribly ironic understanding of Flaubert's style? A style in which
"toutes les parties de la réalité sont converties en une même substance, aux vastes surfaces, d'un miroitement monotone. . . . Tout
ce qui était différent a été converti et absorbé" (all the elements
of reality have been converted into one unanimous substance, into
vast, unvaryingly gleaming surfaces. . . . Everything that was different has been converted and absorbed)?[36]
But before the particular story of Bouvard and Pécuchet can
come to an end, indeed before the Copy can be given its final and
quasi-narrative form, Flaubert himself will come to an untimely
end. *Bouvard et Pécuchet*—and in this it is perhaps exemplary of
all prose, according to Flaubert[37]—remains suspended in a state of
literal incompletion. Guy de Maupassant, Flaubert's disciple and

protégé who will tend both to the body of Flaubert (it is he who washes and dresses Flaubert's body) and to the eight-inch pile of notes left behind for the second volume of *Bouvard et Pécuchet*, sees an intimate connection between the writing of the book and the death of the man:

[L]'œuvre [*Bouvard et Pécuchet*] . . . était de celles qu'on n'achève point. Un livre pareil mange un homme, car nos forces sont limitées et notre effort ne peut être infini. Flaubert écrivit deux or trois fois à ses amis: "J'ai peur que la terminaison de l'homme n'arrive avant celle du livre— ce serait une belle fin de chapitre."

Ainsi qu'il l'avait écrit, il est tombé, un matin, *foudroyé* par le travail, comme un Titan trop audacieux qui aurait voulu monter trop haut.

Et, puisque je suis dans les comparaisons mythologiques, voici l'image qu'éveille en mon esprit l'histoire de Bouvard et Pécuchet.

J'y revois l'antique fable de Sisyphe: ce sont deux Sisyphes modernes et bourgeois qui tentent sans cesse l'escalade de cette montagne de la science, en poussant devant eux cette pierre de la compréhension qui sans cesse roule et retombe.

Mais eux, à la fin, haletants, découragés, s'arrêtent, et, tournant le dos à la montagne, se font un siège de leur rocher. (GM 286, my emphasis)

[T]he book . . . was one of those that cannot be finished. A book of this sort devours a man, for our strength is limited and our effort cannot be infinite. Two or three times Flaubert wrote to his friends: "I am afraid that the end of the man may come before the end of the book—which would make for a fine chapter break."

Just as he had written it, so he fell one morning, *struck down* by his work, like an overbold Titan who had ventured to climb too high.

And, since I am already engaged in mythological comparisons, here is the image that the story of Bouvard and Pécuchet awakens in my mind.

In it, I see the ancient fable of Sisyphus: they are two modern, bourgeois Sisyphus's who constantly try to climb the mountain of science, pushing before them the stone of comprehension that constantly rolls and falls back.

However, in the end, panting, discouraged, they stop and, turning their backs on the mountain, make a seat for themselves on their rock.

But the last word of *Bouvard et Pécuchet*, Maupassant concedes, is missing—

> Ce surprenant édifice de science... devait avoir un couronnement, une conclusion, une justification éclatante. Après ce réquisitoire formidable, l'auteur avait entassé une *foudroyante* provision de preuves, le dossier des sottises cueillies chez les grands hommes. (GM 298, my emphasis)

> This surprising scientific edifice... was supposed to have a crowning achievement, a conclusion, an explosive justification. After such a formidable indictment, the author had accumulated a *devastating* supply of evidence, the dossier of stupidities culled from the mouths of great men.

The last word is missing, unless, that is to say, "foudroyant" is the last word, for it is Maupassant's chosen word—he who observed the body in its final convulsion—to describe Flaubert's end (GM 279; 286; 322; 329): "Puis, j'ai vu, au dernier jour, étendu sur un large divan, un grand mort au cou gonflé, à la gorge rouge, terrifiant comme un colosse *foudroyé*" (Then, on the last day, I saw it, laid out on a wide sofa, the body of a large man with a swollen neck, whose throat was red, terrifying like a colossus that had been *struck down*) (GM 329, my emphasis).

"Foudroyé [*struck down*]" as one is stuck down by lightning but also "ébahi," dumbfounded, as one is dumbfounded by a work of art, according to Flaubert.[38] Although Flaubert's notes and scenarios may indicate that the Copy's lists and enumerations were to be the final result of Bouvard and Pécuchet's encyclopedic quest (their striving for "maximum substance"[39]), it would be wrong to read this projected finality as closure. For a bit of— call it "material irony"—slips in to the novel to ensure that this striving remains *permanently* heterogeneous to the recuperative force of the "trottoir roulant." Flaubert's death, one might say, imposes itself as the decisive textual excess in terms of which his "trottoir roulant" delivers up a terribly ironic and non-figurative blank. Although this blank is immediately recuperated by the editor—"Ici s'arrête le manuscrit de

Gustave Flaubert" (Here ends the manuscript of Gustave Flaubert) (BP 409; 343)—one thing is clear: the shift from a teleological to a tautological model of time in *Bouvard et Pécuchet*, from the impersonal narrative of the first ten chapters to the eight-inch pile of notes, lists, citations of the virtual second volume literally comes to us as a testamentary disruption, as a narrative blank monumentalized by an editorial present: "Ici s'arrête."

This performative utterance registers an event: "Ici" marks the spot, the blank, the space in Chapter 10 where the "trottoir roulant" literally encounters a ghostly present, namely the "posthumous present" of Flaubert's final notes for *Bouvard et Pécuchet*:

> Ainsi tout leur a craqué dans les mains.
> Ils n'ont plus aucun intérêt dans la vie.
> Bonne idée nourrie en secret par chacun d'eux. Ils se la dissimulent – De temps à autre, ils sourient, quand elle leur vient; —puis se la communiquent simultanément: copier.
> Confection du bureau à double pupitre....
> Achat de registres—et d'ustensiles, sandaraque, grattoirs, etc.
>
> Ils s'y mettent. (BP 414)

> Thus everything has come to pieces in their hands.
> They no longer have any interest in life.
> A good idea cherished in secret by each of them. They hide it from one another – From time to time they smile when it occurs to them, —then at last communicate it simultaneously: to copy.
> Manufacture of a two-seated desk....
> Purchase of books—and utensils, sand-sprinklers, erasers, etc.
>
> They set to work. (BP 347–48)

The book Flaubert calls his "testament" ends in a present tense whose power lies in the very unexpectedness of its occurrence. I can do no more than suggest here that this posthumous present, the power of death, as it imposes itself on every reader of *Bouvard et Pécuchet*, constitutes a terribly ironic event of difference in the midst of a story of indifferentiation. A difference (the space and time of a death) emerges here from the shock of the present tense. The relentless force of indifferentiation, the machine-like impassibility of Flaubert's "trottoir roulant" leaves us not with a body, in the end, but with the event of a death—not with a death described in realistic terms, but with the living force of a testament. And one cannot help but wonder whether the event of this posthumous present is not already the language of futurity, futurity, or what Mallarmé will call the "disparition élocutoire qui laisse l'initiative aux mots."

Postscript

Last Words

In these pages I have pointed to what might be termed a hetero-dynamic or force of otherness that lies at the heart of the most foundational concepts of the human. Whether one analyzes Kant's principle of autonomy, Freud's theory of consciousness, or Flaubert's models of temporality, there appears an irreducible something – "absolute heteronomy" (Chapter 1), "the trauma of reality" (Chapter 2), "the posthumous present" (Chapter 3)—whose very emergence on the scene opens the human to forces of dispossession that threaten its very conceptual possibility. This emergence, or the fact that the terms used to define the human depend on elements that are no longer human properly speaking (absolute heteronomy, traumatic reality, death), cannot be eliminated. Because these elements are indifferent or irreducible to any desire, they are often equated with what terrorizes desire: acts of cruelty, wanton violence, that is, with those things we condemn—or monstrosize—as "inhuman." And yet, as I have tried to show in this book, these inhuman elements simultaneously bequeath to us a future insofar as they promise us possibility beyond the possibilities of cognition. The inhuman is our future, I argue, not because we must learn to tolerate violence and atrocity but because the future would have no life without the risk of a certain inhumanity.

Nowhere has the question of inhumanity been as central a concern to the study of literary and philosophical texts than in the work of Paul de Man and Jacques Derrida where it is inextricably linked to the problem of language. There can be no use of language, says de Man, which is not "radically formal, i.e. mechanical, no matter how deeply this aspect may be concealed by aesthetic, formalistic delusions."[1] Language, de Man explains, will always include "the moment of dispossession in favor of the arbitrary power of the play of the signifier," which, from the point of view of the subject— from the point of view of the human—can only be experienced as "a dismemberment, a beheading or a castration" (AR 296). De Man will often associate this arbitrariness of language or that which in language operates independently of and beyond any human desire with a feeling of terror: the experience of threat, cruelty, suffering in dismemberment, decapitation, disfiguration, or castration. Yet it is language's power of dispossession, its power of desubjectivation— the inhuman elements that threaten the integrity of what we call "the human"—that also generate the very possibility of literature.

For Derrida this moment of disposession will be in its essence a passage between language and history, a passage that gestures beyond itself: to the eventness of the event, on the one hand, and to history as inscription on the other.

I

The link between language and eventness (historicity) emerges specifically in de Man in the process that takes us from language as constative or trope (in which language states or describes something) to language as performative (in which language does something). In his 1983 Messenger lecture entitled "Kant and Schiller" and delivered at Cornell just before his death, de Man begins by insisting on the question of irreversibility in the movement from trope to performative, that is, in the passage from a cognitive model of language to another model of language in which language is no longer cognitive:

> [T]he transition, the passage from the conception of language as a system, perhaps a closed system of tropes, that totalizes itself as a series

of transformations which can be reduced to tropological systems, and then the fact that you *pass* from that conception of language to *another* conception of language. . . . That process . . . is irreversible.[2]

The movement from trope to performative, says de Man, goes in one direction and one direction only—and there is no getting back: "you cannot get back from the one to the one before" (AI 133). This process is irreversible and yet, as de Man also says, the process will always be recuperated.

Although the transition from trope to performative is something that "occurs materially," something that "leaves a trace on the world" (AI 132), the performative function of language, de Man tells us, will never be "accepted and admitted" as such:

> [I]t will always be *recuperated*, it will relapse, so to speak, by a kind of reinscription of the performative in a tropological system of cognition again. That relapse, however, is not the same as a reversal. Because this is in turn open to a critical discourse similar to the one that has taken one from the notion of trope to that of the performative. So it is not a return to the notion of trope and to the notion of cognition; it is equally balanced between both, and equally poised between both, and as such is not a reversal, it's a relapse. And a relapse in that sense is not the same; it has to be distinguished in a way which I am only indicating here but which would require much more refined formulation—the recuperation, the relapse, has to be distinguished from a reversal. (AI 133)

However irreversible the passage out of cognition may be, there will always be recuperation. And yet, says de Man, this recuperation or relapse will not return us to an earlier notion of trope. A relapse is not the same as a reversal. Unlike a reversal, a relapse remains "equally balanced" between a mode which is that of cognition and one which is not that of cognition, "equally poised between both." The difference between a relapse and a reversal lies in the mark or scar, residue or remainder that this irreversible passage out of cognition leaves on cognition. De Man's insistence on irreversibility thus points to the impossibility of erasing that moment in language where something like history happens.

II

In his extraordinary commentary on de Man in "Typewriter Ribbon," Derrida takes up de Man's strange notion of "history" that immediately follows his discussion of irreversibility and recuperation in "Kant and Schiller." In the passage concerning history that interests Derrida, de Man argues that history should not be confused with a dialectical movement or with any kind of continuum (whether progressive or regressive) that would be accessible to a cognition. History has nothing at all to do with a temporal process. Here is the passage that Derrida quotes:

> There is history from the moment that words such as "power" and "battle" and so on emerge on the scene. At that moment things *happen*, there is *occurrence*, there is *event*. History is therefore not a temporal notion, it has nothing to do with temporality, but it is the emergence of a language of power out of a language of cognition. (AI 133)

In de Man's "hyperbolic provocation," says Derrida, a temporal unfolding is not the essential predicate of the concept of history. Historicity is not linked to time or to the temporal process but "to power, to the language *of* power and to language *as* power."[3] In this sense, says Derrida, history must be thought as an event of discontinuity, an irreversible disruption, a "revolutionary caesura, or even the end of history, at least of history as teleological process" (TR 320).

But just as de Man's notion of history is bound up with the passage out of cognition and irreversibility so, Derrida insists, is it bound up with the question of inscription:

> De Man constructs his concept of the event, of history as the eventness of events rather than as temporal process, on the basis of two determinations that are equally important for us: that of irreversibility . . . and that of inscription or material trace. (TR 320)

Inscription is essential because it makes indelible the eventness of the event. And because it is a material trace, inscription remains forever legible. How indeed, one might read Derrida as asking here, does one *pass on* a passage out of cognition? But before we can address the passing on of the passage out of cognition another question, this time about a textual passage, arises. For Derrida's quotations from de Man's "Kant and Schiller" essay occur in the middle of another discussion in which Derrida is musing over de Man's strange omission of two small words from his quotation of a passage in Rousseau. Bracketing Derrida's entire discussion of "Kant and Schiller" in "Typewriter Ribbon," in other words, is a discussion of "two little words" (TR 317) that de Man wittingly/unwittingly leaves out of Rousseau's text. This larger discussion becomes all the more interesting to us when we notice that in commenting on de Man in "Kant and Schiller" (a commentary that thus emerges from and returns to a discussion of Rousseau) Derrida adds exactly two little words to his quotation of de Man.

What is more, Derrida's translation of de Man's text adds these two little words exactly at the point of passage *out of* cognition. Here is the passage from de Man that Derrida quotes:

> There is history from the moment that words such as "power" and "battle" and so emerge on the scene. At that moment things *happen*, there is *occurrence*, there is *event*. History is therefore not a temporal notion, it has nothing to do with temporality, but it is the emergence of a language of power out of a language of cognition.

And here is the French in which it is quoted:

> Il y a histoire dès le moment où des mots tels que "pouvoir" et "bataille," etc. apparaissent sur la scène. À ce moment-là les choses *arrivent*, il y a *occurrence*, il y a *événement*. L'histoire n'est donc pas une notion temporelle, elle n'a rien à voir avec la temporalité mais l'émergence d'un langage de pouvoir hors [ou au-delà] d'un langage de la cognition.[4]

"[T]he emergence of a language of power out of a language of cognition" becomes in Derrida's text "l'émergence d'un langage de pouvoir hors [ou au-delà] d'un langage de la cognition." The addition of a bracket and the suggestion of an alternative translation of "out of" delays the passage out of cognition, for it quite literally cuts off the flow of the line—both visually by inserting vertical lines and semantically by separating the prepositional phrase from its object. The effect of Derrida's bracket is to dwell on the movement of translation—the movement of passage—"from [*depuis*]" a language of cognition to a language of power.

There is something decidedly de Manian about this ironic turn in Derrida: one might say that by dwelling on the translation of "out of," by lingering on the emergence of a language of power *out of* a language of cognition, Derrida reads de Man with new emphasis, and that it is this shift, this accentuation, these two little words that change everything. For to dwell on the translation of this idiomatic phrase is not only to address the question of passage (that of passing from English to French), it is also, literally, to remain suspended one moment longer *between* a mode which is that of cognition and a mode which is not that of cognition.

If the passage out of a language of cognition is a single-directed movement that cannot be represented as a temporal process, if between the tropological and the performative there is a separation that allows for no mediation whatsoever, then it becomes imperative, I will argue, to distinguish between two events. On the one hand, there is the historical event (which may in fact be a "textual event"), an event which, as we have seen, is bound to be recuperated; on the other hand, there is the event of a recuperation that fails to reverse the passage out of cognition and thus remains suspended, no longer and not again historical. These two events are not the same event even if they are contemporaneous with one another. The movement of recuperation (or "relapse") reinscribes the historical event in time (i.e. in a "tropological system of cognition"). Such a reinscription necessarily diverges from and in fact recuperates the very thing, which, as de Man says, has "nothing to do with temporality" (KS 133). And yet every historical event as such generates a recuperative movement of this sort, an event insofar as it fails to reverse and therefore conveys the material trace of history. What this means is that it is the second event—namely the movement of recuperation and its failure—that bequeaths any properly historical event to posterity.

III

By suspending the historicity of the event, the movement of recuperation and its failure carry the promise of histories to come. The event of recuperation, that is to say, the failure to reverse the passage out of cognition, is what ensures that history has a history—a future. And yet the movement of recuperation has a machine-like quality to it, for no matter how irreversible the passage out of cognition may be, de Man tells us, there is always recuperation: the language of power "will *always* be reinscribed within a cognitive system, it will *always* be recuperated" (KS 133, my emphasis). History will *always* be accompanied by the attempt and failure to reverse its occurrence. This is because the event of recuperation is built into the historical event; it is internal to it as a necessary and inevitable moment. Paradoxically, thus, one might speak of recuperation as a kind of power of repetition: a power that always—inescapably, predictably, endlessly—tries and fails to return us to an earlier notion of cognition.

But does the inevitability of the movement of recuperation not make impossible the "eventness" of recuperation? How indeed, as Derrida asks in "Typewriter Ribbon," can we even begin to think an "event-machine" (TR 278)?

> One of our greatest difficulties, then, would be to reconcile with the machine a thinking of the event (the real, undeniable, inscribed, singular event, of an always essentially traumatic type . . . inasmuch as its singularity interrupts an order and rips apart . . . the normal tissue of temporality or history). How is one to reconcile, *on the one hand,* a thinking of the event . . . and, *on the other hand,* a certain concept of machine-ness [*machinalité*]? . . . In a word and repeating myself in a quasi-machine-like fashion, how is one to think together the machine *and* the event, a machine-like repetition *and* that which happens? (TR 336)

Not only would the "event-machine" arrive as a new logical form, an unheard of concept, says Derrida—it would threaten the very essence of the event. Could an event that was necessary and foreseeable still be an event? If the eventness of the event requires the fortuitous, the contingent, the unforeseeable, is an "event-machine" not an impossible concept? And yet, says Derrida, by virtue of its very inconceivability, the "event-machine" is "the only and the first possible event, because im-possible" (TR 278). But how are we to read this "im-possibility," an "im-possibility" that exceeds all philosophical determination of the possible by passing out of (or beyond) possibility?

IV

It is here, I will suggest, that we must remember the writing-machine ("je suis un homme-plume," Flaubert writes to Louise Colet in 1852)—who set himself the impossible task of writing a free-standing, authorless book, a book with no external attachment that would hold itself up by the internal force of its style. Indeed, nowhere in the history of Western literature, as I have suggested in this book, does the word-concept machine become so strangely fused with the notion of event than in the work of Gustave Flaubert. From the moment of its publication and prosecution by the legal authorities of the Second Empire in 1857, *Madame Bovary* has signified a shocking literary event.

But what is it in *Madame Bovary* that shocks the reader? The novelist and critic Barbey d'Aurevilly, who would later become one of Flaubert's most vicious critics, writes what is perhaps one of the most penetrating reviews of *Madame Bovary* where he notes, in order precisely to caution against it, Flaubert's machine-ness:

> It is a book . . . without tenderness. . . . M. Flaubert is a man without emotion; he does not judge, at least in any appreciable way. He is a relentless, tireless narrator, an analyst who never gets flustered, a *descriptor* down to the most painstaking detail. However, he is deaf and mute of impression to all that he recounts. He is indifferent to what he writes with the scrupulousness of a lover. Were one to forge narrating-analyzing machines in Birmingham or Manchester out of good English steel, machines that could function on their own by means of an unknown mechanism, they would function exactly in

the same way as M. Flaubert. One would feel in these machines just as much life, soul, human depth as in the man of marble who wrote *Madame Bovary* with a pen of stone, like the knife of savages.

It is repellant to human nature to have a subject without feeling passionately either for or against it. However, M. Flaubert escapes a custom that seems to be a law of the human spirit.

Personally, I know of no literary composition whose talent is truer and at the same time more devoid of enthusiasm, more empty of heart.[5]

"Relentless," "tireless," "indifferent" are the adjectives used to describe the narrating, analyzing, pathos-less machine or the "style" of Flaubert. Marcel Proust will agree with this assessment when he says that it is impossible for whoever has once set foot on "the great moving walkway that are the pages of Flaubert [*ce grand trottoir roulant que sont les pages de Flaubert*]" not to recognize that they are without precedent in literary history. The literary event that is Flaubert, in other words, is inseparable from the narrating, analyzing machine that emerges on the scene with *Madame Bovary*.

And yet it is not until *Bouvard et Pécuchet*, as I have argued, that Flaubert begins to fear that his project has become "radically impossible in its conception" ("J'ai peur qu'il ne soit par sa conception même, radicalement impossible" [GS 479]). This is because the full force of the narrating, analyzing machine only enters into the novel with *Bouvard et Pécuchet*. For the first time, in the novel Flaubert refers to in his letters as his "testament," the monotonous, unrelenting force of the "moving walkway" becomes the allegorical subject of the novel and the scriveners the figure of the writing-machine. Flaubert had originally projected a second volume for *Bouvard et Pécuchet* that would have been composed entirely of his own reading notes for *Bouvard et Pécuchet*: thus *Bouvard et Pécuchet* was to have produced the "Copy" of the two clerks, namely the very material that had produced *Bouvard et Pécuchet*. In this way, the two scriveners would have succeeded in writing their author out of existence; a writing-machine would have produced a work of literature, an unheard-of literary event.

We know the end of the story, however. Flaubert dies before he can finish *Bouvard et Pécuchet*, leaving behind an eight-inch pile of notes for the "Copy." Yet death in this context is a terrible irony, for death itself becomes an event—an event of dispossession produced by and through writing. By failing to complete his project, Flaubert forces us to think the im-possibility of a narrating machine *and* a performative utterance. I would suggest that no matter what else they say, Flaubert's last recorded words for *Bouvard et Pécuchet*—because they speak to us in the present—also say the following: "I give and bequeath you the death of Gustave Flaubert."

Insofar as death and dispossession are events, they are opposed to the notion of cognition. And yet insofar as both events will inevitably be recuperated as figures for what has been called the performative power of language, they will be reinscribed within a cognitive system. As we have seen, however, such machine-like recuperation will always fail to reverse the irreversible passage that constitutes them as events: and in the end, it is this failure that forever marks recuperation for the future—as a conceptual impossibility (history) waiting to happen (again).

I have used the term "legacy" in this book to refer to the irreversible passage out of cognition which, whatever its function, is both irreducible to and inseparable from what we call "the human." As I have tried to show in this book, every legacy points to a structural predicament that forever prevents what we call "epistemology" from closing itself off in spatiotemporal terms. It is my hope that this book will contribute to a rethinking of futurity in terms not of human desire but of history's inhumanity that, whether we like it or not, is "henceforth always in abeyance."[6]

Notes

Introduction: Of Human Bondage

1. Sigmund Freud, *The Future of an Illusion*, SE 21:87; *Die Zukunft einer Illusion, Gesammelte Werke,* 18 vols. (Frankfurt am Main: Fischer Verlag, 1999), 14, 377. Henceforth all references to the German will be to this edition and will not be given in the text.

2. Ironically, Rome is for Freud not just another example of a city, the existence of which can be verified empirically. For Freud, Rome is the figure par excellence of the preservation of memory-traces in the unconscious:

> Now let us, by a flight of imagination, suppose that Rome is not a human habitation but a psychical entity with a similarly long and copious past—an entity, that is to say, in which nothing that has once come into existence will have passed away and all the earlier phases of development continue to exist along the latest one. This would mean that in Rome the palaces of the Caesars and the Septizonium of Septimus Severus would still be rising to their old height on the Palatine and that the castle of S. Angelo would still be carrying on its battlements the beautiful statues which graced it until the siege by the Goths, and so on. (SE 21: 75)

3. Or, as we read in Kant: "Es ist so bequem, unmündig zu sein! [It is so convenient to be immature!]" (Auf 33; 54).

4. Feeling presupposes sensibility, hence the sensuousness and finitude of human beings. In his *Kant und das Problem der Metaphysik* Heidegger precisely forgets that reason does not feel. See in particular "The Transcendental Power of Imagination and Practical Reason" (§30) in Martin

Heidegger, *Kant und das Problem der Metaphysik* (Frankfurt am Main: Klostermann, 1973), 156–60; *Kant and the Problem of Metaphysics*, trans. Richard Taft (Bloomington: Indiana University Press, 1997), 109–12.

5. Henry Allison uses this expression to describe Kant's characterization of the principle of sufficient reason in Kant's discussion of the cosmological conflict of reason with itself. See Henry Allison, "The Antinomy of Pure Reason," *Kant's Transcendental Idealism* (New Haven: Yale University Press, 1983), 53. In *Der Satz vom Grund*, Heidegger draws the connection between pure reason and the principle of sufficient reason understood as *ratio*, on the one hand; and between speculative reason and the principle of sufficient reason (of objects), on the other: "Concealed behind the formula 'a priori conditions of possibility' is the indication [*Zustellung*] of sufficient reason, of *ratio sufficiens*, which, as *ratio*, is pure reason" (126); "The critical question of the sufficient reason of objects becomes the question of the a priori conditions of the possibility of the representation of objects in experience" (132). See in particular lectures nine and ten in *Der Satz vom Grund* (Pfullingen: Neske, 1957), 117–42. For Kant's formulation of the principle of reason, see Immanuel Kant, *Critique of Pure Reason,* trans. Norman Kemp Smith (New York: St. Martin's Press, 1965), A 314 / B 370. For Kant's response to a Leibnizian position on the principle of reason, see Henry Allison, *The Kant–Eberhard Controversy* (Baltimore: Johns Hopkins University Press, 1973).

6. For a radical rethinking of "borders" in the Kantian context, see Geoffrey Bennington's excellent study: Geoffrey Bennington, *Frontières kantiennes* (Paris: Galilée, 2000).

7. In his 1983 Messenger lecture entitled "Kant and Schiller," Paul de Man describes history as just such an emergence. See Paul de Man, "Kant and Schiller," *Aesthetic Ideology* (Minneapolis: University of Minnesota Press, 1996), 133.

1. The Legacy of the Future: Kant and the Ethical Question

1. In an effort to dispel this strangeness, it has been rightly noted that Kant himself never uses the locution "Copernican revolution" to refer to his own change of point of view. Unfortunately, this absence is used primarily to defuse the force of Kant's analogy, such that the reference to Copernicus becomes no more than all too uncomplicated allusion to a similar case in which an alternative hypothesis is sought because an earlier theory proved unsatisfactory. See for example Norwood Russell Hanson, "Copernicus's Role in Kant's Revolution," *JHI* 20 (1959): 274–81.

2. For a strong and very original indictment of Kant along these lines, see in particular Jean Laplanche, "Ponctuation: La révolution copernicienne inachevée," *La révolution copernicienne inachevée* (Paris: Aubier, 1992), iii–xxxv. For an analysis of the figure of Copernicus in Kant's writings, see Friedrich Kaulbach, "Die Kopernikanische Denkfigur bei Kant," *Kant-Studien* 64 (1973): 30–48.

3. Sigmund Freud, "A Difficulty in the Path of Psychoanalysis," *The Standard Edition of the Complete Psychological Works of Sigmund Freud,* trans. James Strachey in collaboration with Anna Freud, assisted by Alix Strachey and Alan Tyson, 24 vols. (London: The Hogarth Press, 1953–1974), 17, 136–44. The Copernican is the first of three blows (*Kränkungen*) inflicted on human narcissism by science. The first blow is cosmological or Copernican (the earth is no longer the center of the universe); the second blow is biological or Darwinian (human beings are of animal descent); the third—"and probably the most wounding"—is of course Freud's own, which is "psychological in nature" (141). Freud concludes this essay with one of his several ambivalent gestures toward philosophy (and to the philosophy of Schopenhauer in particular). Kant is nowhere mentioned, but I will already suggest here—as I will argue further in this chapter—that the Kantian turn, the Kantian revolution may be so revolutionary as to be unrecognizable in terms of "blows" or "narcissism," that is, in terms of any traditional notion of power or selfhood.

4. It should be noted that the adjective "widersinnisch" reappears along with Copernicus's name in Kant's last major published work: see "Renewed Question: 'Is the Human Race Constantly Progressing Toward the Better?'" in *The Conflict of the Faculties* (1798). In this text, however, it is associated not with Copernicus's hypothesis but with that from which the Copernican hypothesis rescues us: "Perhaps the difficulty lies in our incorrect choice of standpoint from which we see the course of human things such that these seem to us so counter to the senses [*widersinnisch*]. The planets, seen from the earth, at times go backward, at times stand still, at times go forward. But taking the standpoint of the sun, which only reason can do, they constantly go forward in their regular path, according to the Copernican hypothesis" (SF 149; 83). Thus "widersinnisch" is the "Art" of Copernicus and just as importantly that state of confusion or disorientation, that "incorrect choice of standpoint" from which his hypothesis rescues us. This reversal marks both the success of the Copernican "Umänderung" (it has achieved the ultimate position of sense-giving hypothesis) but also its failure to affect the pre-revolutionary opposition between that which appears to be "widersinnisch" and that

which is potentially true. Kant's revolution on the other hand, I will argue, as the revolution of revolutions, will affect even this most fundamental of oppositions.

5. I am freely translating two terms that Kant uses to describe the reasons why human beings fall such easy prey to intellectual intuition: "Es liegt nämlich nicht bloß in der natürlichen Trägheit sondern auch in der Eitelkeit der Menschen (einer mißverstandenen Freiheit) [It lies not merely in the natural laziness but also in the vanity of human beings (a misunderstood freedom)]" (Ton 390; 52). In this text, Kant associates a language of *desire* with the oracular mysticism of the Neo-Platonists who resemble nothing so much as sophists in the guise of philosophers.

6. It should be noted that this summons has nothing of the divine or inspired about it. Indeed, although I will do no more than point to an instance of it here, this voice may suddenly emerge from something as mundane as an agrammatical construction: "Und bei einem solchen Ver-fahren hat uns die spekulative Vernunft zu solcher Erweiterung immer doch wenigstens Platz vershafft, wenn *sie* ihn gleich leer lassen mußte, und es bleibt uns also noch unbenommen, ja wir sind gar dazu durch *sie* aufgefordert, ihn durch praktische Data *derselben,* wenn wir können, auszufüllen" (B xxi-ii, my emphasis). The surprising shift through a very elusive grammatical play between a first "sie" whose antecedent is without question "die spekulative Vernunft," a second "sie" whose antecedent is both grammatically restricted to "die spekulative Vernunft" and referen-tially (but only retrospectively) dependent on "die [reine] Vernunft" and the appearance of "derselben" whose antecedent can be nothing other than "die Vernunft": thus, although grammar mechanically pushes for-ward our understanding and imposes a symmetrical antecedent construc-tion on the two instances of "sie," an unanticipated referential encounter awaits us in "derselben," for the antecedent here can no longer be any-thing but "die [reine] Vernunft." Grammar confounds us by making a second demand that is incompatible with the first: either the antecedent of the second "sie" is "die spekulative Vernunft," and the pronoun "der-selben" constitutes the moment or the place of the agrammatical turn; or it is the second "sie" that is itself this place. The more one reads or rereads this passage in Kant, the more impossible becomes this shift, which can be captured neither in the first "sie" nor in the second "sie." And yet this shift occurs quite easily and naturally—unconsciously—insofar as we understand what Kant is saying. However, it is precisely this step from speculative reason to pure reason that the *Critique of Pure Reason* itself

critiques. In understanding this "simple" agrammatical construction, in other words, we have understood nothing of the critique of pure reason.

7. Kant's own notion of "Evolution," which he distinguishes from "Revolution" in *The Conflict of the Faculties*, is still far too promising (and thus far less radical) than what I have in mind here. Revolution may promise nothing (at least nothing that might be taken as a sign of human progress) but nonetheless change everything (at least insofar as grounds are concerned): such a revolution would be a revolution without "battlefield," without hostility, one whose force may be invisible—like the Newtonian attraction—but whose necessity (and not simply whose necessary hypothesis) is irrefutable. For a radical reading of "Evolution" in Kant, see Peter Fenves, *A Peculiar Fate: Metaphysics and World-History in Kant* (Ithaca: Cornell University Press, 1991), 239–85.

8. Henry Allison, *Kant's Theory of Freedom* (Cambridge: Cambridge University Press, 1990), 100.

9. Ibid., 97. I will not take up here Kant's problematic move from negative to positive conceptions of freedom nor will I engage his argument in the Third Section of the *Grundlegung* and further in the *Critique of Practical Reason* that autonomy is not only a necessary condition for the possibility of moral law but also its sufficient condition: "a free will and a will subject to moral laws are one and the same" (Gr 447; 49). For further discussion of these points see Henry Allison, "The Reciprocity Thesis" in *Kant's Theory of Freedom*, 201–13, and "Autonomy and Spontaneity in Kant's Conception of the Self," *Idealism and Freedom* (Cambridge: Cambridge University Press, 1996), 129–42.

10. Kant's most remarkable response to this human dilemma lies, I would suggest, in his Postulates.

11. These two particular terms, which I have selected from the literature, seem to me symptomatic of a generalized (but perhaps predominantly Anglo-American) tendency in Kant criticism.

12. See Paul de Man, "Semiology and Rhetoric," *Allegories of Reading: Figural Language in Rousseau, Nietzsche, Rilke, and Proust* (New Haven: Yale University Press, 1979), 4.

13. By no means should this be construed as a repudiation of theory, for theory is necessary and good for life. Indeed such recuperation would correspond to the Kantian notion of *Erkennistrieb* or cognitive drive, which, like moral feeling, is a pure product of reason and which, because it is a natural inclination, cannot be extirpated, nor should it be (see "What is Orientation in Thinking?"). In commenting on the similarity

between the Analytics of the first and second *Critiques,* Kant says the following in the *Critique of Practical Reason:* "Whoever has been able to convince himself of the truth of the propositions of the Analytic will get a certain enjoyment out of such comparisons, for they correctly occasion the expectation of bringing some day into view the unity of the entire pure rational faculty (both theoretical and practical) and of being able to derive everything from one principle. The latter is an unavoidable need of human reason [*das unvermeidliche Bedürfnis der menschlichen Vernunft*], as it finds complete satisfaction only in a systematic unity of its cognitions" (KprV 90–91; 94). But neither should we forget the words of Charcot to Freud that Freud is so fond of citing: "La théorie, c'est bon, mais ça n'empêche pas d'exister."

14. Paul de Man, "Kant's Materialism," *Aesthetic Ideology,* ed. Andrzej Warminski (Minneapolis: University of Minnesota Press, 1996), 128.

15. For a reading of futurity as the renewal of a question that is not directed toward an answer but rather toward a movement of endless repetition, see Peter Fenves, *A Peculiar Fate: Metaphysics and World-History in Kant* (Ithaca: Cornell University Press, 1991).

16. Allison, *Kant's Theory of Freedom,* 97.

17. I have used the neuter case to translate all references to rational beings because "Wesen" is a neuter noun in German and, more importantly, because the argument I will make concerning "rational nature" and the structural necessity of an *non-empirical* other is itself a reading of the neuter.

18. In the "Doctrine of Rights" (1797), the distinction between "person [*Person*]" and "thing [*Sache*]" is drawn again, this time in terms of the very possibility of "imputation [*Zurechnung*]" (MS 223; 50). Thus, "a *person* is a subject whose actions can be imputed to him.... A *thing* is that [Sache *ist ein Ding*] to which nothing can be *imputed.*"

19. Just as it is bound to rational nature, the moral law is bound to human nature. The unconditioned practical law needs the human. What is foreign to the human nonetheless requires the human. What is radically heterogeneous to the human is indissociable from the human. This is because "rational nature" and "human nature" are not symmetrical terms. Rational nature is above human nature. But even if it always remains above human nature, rational nature needs the human. This exigency is itself constitutive of rational nature, for moral law could not remain unconditioned—one could not *save* its being unconditioned—were its unconditionality not predicated on a limit, the boundary line of

heteronomy. Moreover, an unconditioned necessity that was not bound to the human would have no positive reality, no life. A causality of freedom, a *modus operandi* that did not have to take effect, that did not have to become actual, concrete, categorical would be lifeless, abstract, illusory, and perfectly inhuman, thus precisely the opposite of what it is for Kant—a driving force in the world, a command. Such abstract autonomy would be without history and without future; it would be but a relative autonomy, the autonomy of the end of time. See J. B. Schneewind, "Autonomy, Obligation, and Virtue: An Overview of Kant's Moral Philosophy," *The Cambridge Companion to Kant*, ed. Paul Guyer (Cambridge: Cambridge University Press, 1992), 309–41. Schneewind's essay on Kant's moral philosophy shows this relation, which he expresses in terms of "form" and "content," to be incontrovertible: "It takes the two working together to produce morality" (318).

20. In *Religion Within the Limits of Reason Alone* (1793), Kant describes the different predispositions of human beings. The predisposition to "humanity" is the capacity of human beings to use reason in the service of inclination; the predisposition to "personality" is "the capacity for respect for the moral law as *in itself sufficient incentive of the will*" (Rel 28; 22–23).

21. To be replaceable in its irreplaceability is the predicament of every singularity according to Jacques Derrida. Indeed the very concept of singularity appeals to what Derrida calls the principle of neutralization (indifference, equivalence, substitution). In the moral realm, says Derrida, this repetition-serialization takes the form of an absolute indifference, an indifference to all particular characteristics: "two human beings *for example* have an equal moral, juridical, political *dignity* whatever their differences in all other respects (social, economic, biological, sexual, psychical, or intellectual, etc.)" See in particular Jacques Derrida, "On the 'Priceless,' or the 'Going Rate' of the Transaction," *Negotiations: Interventions and Interviews 1971–2001*, ed. Elizabeth Rottenberg (Stanford: Stanford University Press, 2001). Without this universalizing principle and neutralizing indifference, in other words, dignity itself, that is, the possibility of singularity, responsibility, decision—everything we call "politics" and "ethics"—would be destroyed. For a truly brilliant and provocative reading of this problem, see Martin Heidegger, *Schellings Abhandlung Über das Wesen der menschlichen Freiheit* (Tübingen: Niemeyer, 1995): "Everything is indifferently the same as any other when we grasp it merely as an 'aliquid,' abstracting from it all content; from this

perspective, as aliquid, every thing is worth (the same as) every other, and we can say: identity as the empty sameness of 'something' with itself is the category of pure indifference, that is of a co-membership (belonging together) that is not and cannot truly be a co-membership as such" (136).

22. What I would like to suggest here is that there exists an inevitable tension between two models of difference. The first is a tropological model or a model by substitution and exchange, which is the one to which Kant must explicitly appeal, and which is based on a knowledge of rational beings and their characteristic—and therefore exchangeable—property, namely their inalienable dignity or singularity. This first model is an infinitesimal and totalizing system in which even a sovereign, indeed a rational sovereign, can be accommodated—"therefore, if one abstracts from the personal differences of rational beings and also from the content of their private ends, then it will be possible to think of a whole of all ends in systematic connection...a kingdom of ends" (Gr 433; 39). The second is a tautological model or a model by enumeration (an endlessly repetitive but non-infinitesimal model that never goes anywhere), which emerges precisely from the first model and according to which difference always ends up pointing to a repetitive and mechanical sameness. What I am arguing is that the unavoidable passage from the first model to the second model requires a moment or space that cannot be accounted for by either model and thus marks for the first time an absolute and unassimilable difference. See Paul de Man's discussion of Baudelaire's "Correspondances" in "Aesthetic Formalization: Kleist's *Über das Marionettentheater*": "The tension, in this poem, occurs indeed between number as trope (the infinitesimal as the underlying principle of totalization) and number as tautology (the stutter of an endless enumeration that never goes anywhere)." Paul de Man, "Aesthetic Formalization: Kleist's *Über das Marionettentheater*," *Rhetoric of Romanticism* (New York: Columbia University Press, 1984), 266.

23. Kant footnotes this proposition, which he puts forward "as a postulate [*Postulat*]" (Gr 429; 36). As Paton remarks in a footnote to Kant's footnote, this proposition refers us to the discussion of the idea of freedom in the Third Section of the *Grundlegung* where Kant claims that a rational being can only act under this idea and therefore must conceive of itself as autonomous, that is, as an end in itself. See *Groundwork of the Metaphysic of Morals*, trans. H. J. Paton (New York: Harper Torchbooks, 1964), 139.

24. This simultaneity should not to be confused with the question of the syntheticity of the moral law. One cannot derive the moral law

from the concept of a rational being (even a perfectly rational one) unless transcendental freedom, the "positive concept of freedom," is also presupposed (Gr 447; 49). Transcendental freedom—the conception of freedom which is required for genuine autonomy—furnishes the third and binding term connecting the concept of an absolutely good will with the requirements of moral law. I cannot address here the many additional complexities involved in linking the possession of reason with the possession of a will. Suffice it to say, as Kant does in the *Grundlegung*, that freedom "holds only as a necessary presupposition of reason in a being that believes itself to be conscious of a will, i.e., of a faculty distinct from mere desire" (Gr 459; 127). Only in the *Critique of Practical Reason* (1788) does the consciousness of obligation finally provide both the concept of free volition and the assurance that for purposes of action such a concept has objective reality. For a discussion of the *Grundlegung's* failure to deduce the practicality of pure reason, see Henry Allison's distinction between a *Verstandeswelt* and an *intelligibelen Welt* in "The Deduction in *Groundwork* III," *Kant's Theory of Freedom*, 214–29. For a critique of Kant's analytic connection between freedom and moral law, see Gerold Prauss, *Kant über Freiheit als Autonomie* (Frankfurt am Main: Klostermann, 1983), 83–100. It may be that Prauss's suggestion of a synthetic connection applies primarily to "human nature" as distinguished from "rational nature." Can it be said that we are free to obey a law just in case we are free to transgress this law? Is a perfectly rational being free to obey the moral law if and only if it is free to defy this law? The perfectly rational being, the being that is *incapable* of acting against the moral law, may indeed be the most free yet at the same time unable to perform many actions that are humanly possible. In this way the moral law, which Kant conceives of as a *modus operandi*, becomes a *modus obligandi* only for rational beings who are imperfectly rational.

25. Infinite difference is not self-difference; it is not a difference determined by a self. It is not a determinate negation.

26. But such a hypothetical will, even for Kant, has no positive reality. Thus we find the following recorded in Vigilantius's notes of 1793: "Like an angel, a being of this kind [a morally perfect being] can in no way be thought of as existing, but to the philosopher is merely an Idea." *Lectures on Ethics*, eds. Peter Heath and J. B. Schneewind, trans. Peter Heath (Cambridge and New York: Cambridge University Press, 1997), 259. God may be the most free but even God is not free of human finitude. In this way, it might be said that the Kant of 1785 has already anticipated the Schelling of 1809.

27. Werner Hamacher, "The Promise of Interpretation: Remarks on the Hermeneutic Imperative in Kant and Nietzsche," *Premises*, trans. Peter Fenves (Cambridge and London: Harvard University Press, 1996), 98. In Hamacher's reading of Kant's imperative as the discovery of finitude, the law is not merely the essence and ground of a thing but also, fundamentally, the demand for this thing. Such a law is thus always and already a *modus obligandi*.

28. As a condition of possibility of moral law qua law, absolute heteronomy is not something we might ever hope to encounter as such in the phenomenal world. Nor is it something we could ever hope to destroy (or murder, as one might a human being), for the imputable "I" of the murderer is already indebted to this condition of possibility. Absolute heteronomy cannot be derived from experience, although, as we will see in the following section, it in no way opposed to the human, for only human reason, it seems, can read the indelible mark it leaves on experience.

29. On "expositives," see J. L. Austin, *How to Do Things with Words* (Cambridge: Harvard University Press, 1962), 155.

30. I can do nothing here but suggest that de Man's mention of "posterity" concerning future readings of Kant's "materialism" is not without relation to this legacy: "The critical power of a transcendental philosophy undoes the very project of such a philosophy leaving us, certainly not with ideology—for transcendental and ideological (metaphysical) principles are part of the same system—but with a materialism that Kant's posterity has not yet begun to face up to. This happens not out of a lack of philosophical energy or rational power, but as a result of the very strength and consistency of this power." See Paul de Man, "Phenomenality and Materiality in Kant," *Aesthetic Ideology*, ed. Andrzej Warminski (Minneapolis: University of Minnesota Press, 1996), 89.

31. Here—but also perhaps paradigmatically—to hear a repetition of sameness *differently* (other-wise). It might be interesting to consider John Rawls's *A Theory of Justice* as both the most Kantian and un-Kantian extension of Kant in which this repetition of sameness is read as radical (self-)sameness; thus Rawls's actors, as Jacqueline Rose remarks in her discussion of justice in *States of Fantasy*, "may be suspended in space and time, but they are absolutely self-identical, utterly *sure* of themselves. His so-called ignorance is disingenuous, not to say knowing, at least about what is going on inside everyone else's head." See Jacqueline Rose, "Just,

Lasting, Comprehensive," *States of Fantasy* (Oxford: Oxford University Press, 1996), 86.

32. The two parts of *The Metaphysics of Morals* were originally published as separate books, the *Doctrine of Right* in early 1797 and the *Doctrine of Virtue* in August of the same year. Kant's reply to a review by Friedrich Bouterwek in the *Göttingen Journal* was later included as an appendix to the *Doctrine of Right* in its 1798 edition.

33. One is reminded here of Paul de Man's discussion of Keats's unfinished epic poem "The Fall of Hyperion" in which it becomes impossible to know how to interpret possession in the title: "Do we have to interpret the genitive in the title . . . as meaning 'Hyperion's Fall,' the case story of the defeat of an older by a newer power, the very recognizable story from which Keats indeed started out but from which he increasingly strayed away, or as 'Hyperion Falling,' the much less specific but more disquieting evocation of an actual falling, regardless of its beginning, its end or the identity of the entity to whom it befalls to be falling?" See Paul de Man, "The Resistance to Theory," *The Resistance to Theory* (Minneapolis: University of Minnesota Press, 1986), 16. Once again, in other words, it may be impossible to decide whether such a passage represents a triumph or a fall.

34. See also the French legal notion of "saisine" (distraint). In article 724 of the French *Civil Code,* we read the following: "Les héritiers légitimes, les héritiers naturels et le conjoint survivant sont saisis de plein droit des biens, droits et actions du défunt, sous l'obligation d'acquitter toutes les charges de la succession. L'État doit se faire envoyer en possession": *Code civil* (Paris: Dalloz, 1977), 380. The important term here is "saisi": those who are "saisis" or "distrained" have what is legally called "la saisine." La saisine goes into effect immediately upon the death of the testator. Hence, there is no legal hiatus, no lapse in the possession of the legacy. The legacy never ceases to belong to someone; there is no discontinuity in the devolution of goods. In French law, furthermore, a subject is declared an heir so long as he/she has not officially renounced the succession. La saisine is not possession; rather, it precedes possession. Where there is neither heir nor legatee the State comes into possession of the goods of the deceased. However, although the State has the capacity to come into possession of the goods, the State does not have the immediate right of "saisine"—"L'État doit se faire envoyer en possession."

35. Kant himself conveys this difficulty by confusing the terms. He will replace one with the other in his discussion of "transfer by contract."

For what his argument literally *means* is "res nullius" but what it *says* is "res vacua": see and compare §20 and §34 in the "Doctrine of Right." The difficulty of maintaining a rigorous distinction between these terms is no accident, I will claim, since what it is trying to articulate is the (im)possibility of passage between rational beings.

36. This prohibition includes for Kant all forms of self-mutilation that reduce humanity to the merely human or corporeal. Humanity represents an integrity that must not be treated or conceived of otherwise than as a singularity. Skills, which have a price, belong to the singularity qua singularity and therefore do not violate this integrity.

37. "Untimeliness" is once again implicated in Kant's account of personhood. One cannot help but be reminded here of the untimely timeliness of Kant's performative declaration in the *Grundlegung*: "Now I say," Kant declared, "that a human being, and in general every rational being, exists as an end in itself" (Gr 428; 35).

38. Kant often remarks that freedom is *schrecklich* or even *entsetzlich*. On freedom and fear in Kant, see Gerold Prauss, *Kant über Freiheit als Autonomie* (Frankfurt am Main: Klostermann, 1983), 145–46. One reader of Kant who took the relation between freedom and fear very seriously indeed was Hegel. See in particular the section "Absolute Freedom and the Terror" in the *Phänomenologie des Geistes*. G. W. F. Hegel, *Werke*, eds. E. Moldenhauer and K. M. Michel (Frankfurt am Main: Suhrkamp, 1970), 3, 431–44. For a brilliant discussion of the term "ent/setzlich" and its infinite implications, see the first chapter of Werner Hamacher's *Premises*, trans. Peter Fenves (Cambridge: Harvard University Press, 1996). In this chapter, Hamacher speaks of the "onto-thesiological structure of metaphysics" and points to the terminological series of "setzen, stellen, legen." See also Hamacher's essay "Affirmative Strike" that is devoted to the reading of one word, "entsetzen": Werner Hamacher, "Affirmative, Strike," in *Walter Benjamin's Philosophy: Destruction and Experience,* eds. Andrew Benjamin and Peter Osbourne, trans. Dana Hollander (London and New York: Routledge, 1994), 110–38.

39. From "Selections from *Notes*, written by Immanuel Kant in his *Observations on the Feeling of the Beautiful and the Sublime*," trans. J. B. Schneewind (private communication).

40. In her translation, Mary Gregor renders this as "someone other." For a critique of such misreadings, see Werner Hamacher's "The Promise of Interpretation: Remarks on the Hermeneutic Imperative in Kant and Nietzsche": "The critique of this metaphor [of the tribunal in §13 of the

"Doctrine of Virtue"] undertaken by Schopenhauer in his Prize-Essay on the *Foundations of Morality* (§9) rests on a fundamental misunderstanding. In particular, the moral self-consciousness that Kant designates as conscience is not, as Schopenhauer . . . suggests, a 'prosopopoeia' for a voice of reason activated in a conventional or utilitarian manner; in accordance with its thoroughly *a priori* and thus non-anthropological argumentation, moral self-consciousness is the representation of 'something other (than man as such)'—therefore precisely not a prosopopoeia but its disruption". Werner Hamacher, *Premises,* trans. Peter Fenves (Cambridge: Harvard University Press, 1996), 106.

41. See Werner Hamacher, *Premises,* trans. Peter Fenves (Cambridge: Harvard University Press, 1996), 105. This is his point, which I am making in slightly different terms.

42. Jacques Derrida, "Deconstruction in America: An Interview with Jacques Derrida," *Critical Exchange* 17 (Winter 1985), 1–33.

2. *Freud: When Morality Makes Us Sick: Disavowal, Ego Splitting, and the Tragedy of Obsessional Neurosis*

1. "In dreams and in neuroses what is thus excluded knocks for admission at the gates." (Sigmund Freud, *Group Psychology and the Analysis of the Ego*)

"If we always return to Freud, it is because of an initial, central intution that is of an ethical order." (Jacques Lacan, *The Ethics of Psychoanalysis*)

2. Freud is defining affect here as "the sum of excitation" with which a representation is "loaded [*behaftet*]" (SE 3: 48).

3. According to a footnote in Section 2 of the "The Neuro-Psychoses of Defense" (SE 3: 51, n. 4), the publication history of this article includes a number of misprints in which the term "unverträglich" (incompatible) is replaced by "unerträglich" (intolerable). This replacement, so it is claimed, is an error, for it is the former term that is found most frequently in Freud's writings of this period. Indeed Freud's use of "inconciliable" in his French article, "Obsessions et Phobies," written at the same time, would seem to confirm this point. According to the Editor's Note to the French article, however, "[t]here has been a good deal of unwillingness to accept this word ['unverträglich'] as meaning 'incompatible'" (SE 3: 72). And, in fact, "intolerable" was finally adopted as the uniform translation in the *Collected Papers* of 1924. One cannot help but wonder what is at

stake in this particular question of translation. The footnote concludes rather unremarkably: "Though no doubt the two words roughly imply the same meaning, they give... different pictures of the psychological situation, a difference which it seems desirable to preserve." I would argue that the shift (intentional? non-intentional?)—which, as we will see, occurs in Freud's own language—between the terms "incompatible" and "intolerable," between what is a mathematical or logical impossibility and what is an experience of this impossibility, points to a threat that is both formal and psychological in nature. In this way, the literal oscillation between the terms marks the place or moment where the two threats converge.

4. In "The Loss of Reality in Neurosis and Psychosis" (SE 10: 182–87), Freud makes clear that the distinction drawn between neurosis and psychosis refers not to the symptoms of a secondary defense but to the situation at the beginning of the illness. Thus, the "loosening of the relation to reality" that is observed in neurosis proper occurs only as a second step, namely as the consequence of those "[secondary] processes which provide a compensation for the portion of the id that has been damaged—that is to say, in the reaction against the repression and in the failure of the repression" (SE 10: 183). In a psychosis, likewise, there are two steps: the first, which drags the ego away from reality, and the second, which has the character of a reparation. In a psychosis, however—and in this it is genetically different from a neurosis—the first step is already pathological and "cannot but lead to illness" (SE 10: 186). The second step, therefore, in both neurosis and psychosis, serves "the desire for power [*Machtbestreben*] of the id," its "displeasure [*Unlust*]" or "incapacity [*Unfähigkeit*]" to adapt itself to reason and necessity (SE 10: 185). Hence, neurosis and psychosis differ from each other in their initial reaction to pathogenic conflict rather than in their secondary attempts at reparation that follow.

5. "But there is a further complication," we read at the very beginning of Chapter 3 in *The Ego and the Id*, the chapter entitled "The Ego and the Super-Ego (Ego Ideal)."

6. The question of what this mechanism may be, says Freud, "cannot... be answered without fresh investigation"; however, he already gives us a clue to what he will later call "disavowal" (*Verleugnung*)—"such a mechanism, it would seem, must, like repression, comprise a withdrawal [*Abziehung*] of the cathexis [*Besetzung*] sent out by the ego" (SE 10: 153).

7. One cannot help but think of the *Grundlegung* here and Kant's recognition of some "foreign impulse [*fremder Antrieb*]" as the source of pathological desire or heteronomy of the will. That this coincidence

should point to a specifically psychoanalytic ethics is what I will now attempt to argue.

8. Sandor Ferenczi will later argue that there exists an intrinsic link between wishing and a narcissistic reality organization. Thus all wishing involves both negative and positive hallucination: "[T]he new-born babe seeks to attain a state of satisfaction merely through insistent wishing (imagining), whereby it simply ignores (represses) the unsatisfying reality, picturing to itself as present, on the contrary, the wished-for, but lacking satisfaction; it attempts, therefore, to conceal without effort all its needs by means of positive and negative hallucinations." Sandor Ferenczi, "Stages in the Development of the Sense of Reality," *First Contributions to Psychoanalysis* (New York: Bruner-Mazel, 1980), 213.

9. One might say, in the language of Winnicott, that "bad enough mothering" is necessary to the proper functioning of the reality principle.

10. Jacques Lacan, "La signification du phallus," *Écrits* (Paris: Éditions du Seuil, 1966), 688.

11. See in particular Samuel Weber, *Return to Freud*, trans. Michael Levine (Cambridge: Cambridge University Press, 1991), 143. See also Edith Jacobson who, in comparing denial (*Verleugnung*, disavowal) to repression (*Verdrängung*), describes the "immediate, painful distortion of reality" that takes place in fetishism: "This outstanding example of denial, the denial of female castration, illuminates the distortion of reality which is regularly involved in this defense. Actually, either of the two opposing ideas distorts realistic facts: even though women do lack a penis, they are certainly not castrated. The child's common misinterpretation of the female genital perceived indeed reveals the direct influence of the id on the initial perception." Edith Jacobson, "Denial and Repression," *J. Amer. Psychoanal. Assn.* 5 (1957): 77.

12. I would suggest here that what is commonly but improperly referred to as "sexual difference," namely the genital difference between male and female, is itself the most primal of fetishistic compromise formations—a fantasized opposition that becomes a static "reality" or an objective "fact," a (natural, historical, political, ideological . . .) fetishization that testifies to a defensive repudiation of the highest order. In this way, the emergence of autoerotism in Freud (the emergence of the sexual drives as such, namely as drives that have become detached from the self-preservative drives) may be read as a defensive, narcissistic response to the trauma of absolute difference. An absolute difference that would be neither sexual nor non-sexual but the condition of possibility of this split. Fetishism—the acknowledgment/refusal of sexual difference as genital

difference—is exemplary precisely to the extent that it registers (and repudiates)—repeats—the sexualization of absolute difference.

13. Three notable exceptions here are J. A. Brook, Humphrey Morris, and Alan Bass. In his 1992 paper "Freud and Splitting," Brook observes: "Freud did not know whether he had something entirely new in this notion of the splitting of the ego, perhaps even as a new way to conceptualize the foundation of all the defenses." See J. A. Brook, "Freud and Splitting," *Int. Rev. Psychoanal.* 13 (1992): 347. In "Narrative, Representation, Narrative Enactment and the Psychoanalytic Construction of History," Morris shows how Freud brings a challenge to his "lifting-of-repression model of history and interpretive understanding" by indicating the constraints that emerge from within this model. Morris points to Freud's late writing on ego splitting in which "the notion of 'original repression' itself seems to give way to something more like original disavowal." See Humphrey Morris, "Narrative, Representation, Narrative Enactment and the Psychoanalytic Construction of History," *Int. J. Psychoanl.* 74 (1993): 34, 47. In Alan Bass's recent work to which I am very much indebted, Bass explores the implications of primary process defense in waking life. "Concrete" patients, he notes, defend against the very process of interpretation (and yet remain in analysis for long periods of time). The process of defense employed by such patients challenges—indeed has always challenged—the centrality of repression in psychoanalytic theory and practice. He argues for a notion of "primary disavowal," which he reads as the registration and repudiation of processive reality (a temporalization of sexual difference); this, in turn, has important implications for clinical practice. See Alan Bass, *Difference and Disavowal: The Trauma of Eros* (Stanford: Stanford University Press, 2000).

14. In his "Notes upon a Case of Obsessional Neurosis" (1909), Freud remarks that obsessional patients often dissimulate their condition as long as they can and only come for treatment when symptoms become very severe, so severe, in fact, that "had they been suffering, for instance, from tuberculosis of the lungs," they would have been refused admission to a sanitarium (SE 10: 157).

15. In the clinical literature, Luther is often considered to be an early example of Obsessive-Compulsive Disorder (OCD): "From 1517, when he first celebrated mass, Luther worried greatly for fear he had carried out some trifling act of omission which would be a sin. Blasphemous thoughts pressed in on him; he wanted to confess several times each day. Eventually his preceptor in the monastery had to discipline him for

this." Judith L. Rapoport, *The Boy Who Couldn't Stop Washing* (New York: Penguin Books, 1990), 240. The Catholic concept of obsessional neurosis or "scrupulosity," Rapoport writes, dates back at least to the twelfth century. The term "scrupulosity" comes from the Latin "scrupus," whose diminutive form "scrupulus" means a small, sharp stone. The neutral "scrupulum" is defined as the smallest division of weight, the twenty-fourth part of an ounce: a minute weight such that it could only tip the scales of a sensitive balance (237).

16. Freud admired Charcot for his theorization of hysteria and in particular, as Jean Laplanche notes, for having taken the hypothesis of "possession" seriously. In 1906, when Freud makes a list of what he takes to be the three most important scientific books, he again reveals his undying interest in questions of possession. The works of Copernicus and Darwin are first and second in this list. However, Freud's third-place choice is quite surprising. In third place, we find a book by Johannes Weier, published in 1563 and entitled *De praestigiis daemonum et incantationibus ac veneficiis (On the Illusions of Demons, Enchantments and Poison Potions)*. In 1917, Freud will make yet another list in which he enumerates the most important blows to have been inflicted on human narcissism by science. The names Copernicus and Darwin are again first and second in this list. The Copernican blow is cosmological (the earth is no longer the center of the universe); the Darwinian blow is biological (human beings are of animal descent). In this list of scientific revolutions, however, the third blow—"and probably the most wounding"—is the blow inflicted on the ego by the discoveries of psychoanalysis (SE 12: 141). Psychoanalysis is the third most important scientific decentering of the human world. And yet, in Freud's original list of scientific books, the place that would correspond to Freud's own work is occupied not by a work of psychoanalysis but by a book on demonic possession. It might be argued, however, as I will in the case of obsessional neurosis, that psychoanalytic writing remains the most advanced, refined, and revolutionary mode of studying possession, that is, of studying the ways in which the ego is not master in its own house. See Jean Laplanche, *Entre séduction et inspiration: l'homme* (Paris: Presses Universitaires de France, 1999), 155–57.

17. Harold Bloom's insight is visionary in this respect: "Jacques Lacan has suggested that the four fundamental concepts of psychoanalysis are the unconscious, the compulsion to repeat, the transference, and the drive. I am not a psychoanalyst, but as an amateur speculator, I would ask whether defense is not the most fundamental concept of psychoanalysis,

and also the most empirically grounded of all Freud's path-breaking ideas? Repression is the center of Freud's vision of man, and when a revised theory of defense broke open the white light of repression into the multi-colored auras of the whole range of defenses, then Freud had perfected an instrument that even psychoanalysis scarcely has begun to exploit." Harold Bloom, "Freud's Concepts of Defense and the Poetic Will," *Sigmund Freud*, ed. Harold Bloom (New York: Chelsea House, 1985), 145.

18. The resonance with Freud's famous phrase is unmistakable here: "Afflavit et dissipati sunt" (he blew on it, and they disappeared).

19. Such that it becomes impossible to decide whether the ego depersonalizes the father because it fears castration or whether castration anxiety arises in order to give the ego an outlet for its personifications.

20. Freud's thinking about the origin and role of the superego is not uniform. In *The Ego and the Id*, Freud seems to draw a parallel between the severity of the superego and the severity of an actual father's prohibition (internalized in the superego). In 1930, however, Freud modifies his theory, following the discoveries of Melanie Klein, as he acknowledges in *Civilization and Its Discontents*. For Klein, not only does there exist no direct correspondence between an actual parent and the infant's superego, the Oedipal drama itself is peopled by personifications of the aggressive drives of the infant. A severe or cruel superego, Freud concedes in *Civilization and Its Discontents*, often corresponds to a benevolent or lenient parent. Thus Freud has modified his theory: although an initial frustration is imposed on the id from without (old theory), experience teaches us (Klein) that the severity of the superego does not correspond to a real model. In the *Outline*, however, as we see here, Freud has returned to a theory in which the superego is again heir to something absolutely external. I will suggest in what follows that this return is not a regression, for Freud is not merely returning to his earlier empiricism.

Although his critique of Freud is very different from Melanie Klein's, Jean-Joseph Goux, like Melanie Klein, must in the end simply presuppose the existence of that which Freud's "Oedipus complex" was supposed to explain. In *Oedipus, Philosopher*, Jean-Joseph Goux notes a series of anomalies that distinguish the Oedipus myth from the typical heroic myth. The myth of Oedipus, according to Goux, is not a myth of paternal interdiction, but rather a myth of the absence of the trial-imposing king. The killing of the father is thus an aberration that takes the place of the conventional act: a challenge issued by a king and accepted by the hero.

Goux argues that by failing to recognize its atypical status as heroic myth, Freud misses the subversive quality of the Oedipus myth:

> By attributing the threat of castration to a strong, angry father who wants to prevent or avenge his son's desire for his (the father's) own wife, Freud unduly humanizes the break; he deprives it of its prehuman, superhuman, inhuman necessity. In this sense . . . he is behaving like Oedipus, who answers the riddle of the Sphinx with the word "man." The initiatory adventure frees the young man from his agonizing and abyssal attraction to the maternal dimension. But the hero's painful and bloody liberation (the severing of the living link with the monster-mother, which can only be experienced as mutilation) does not result from his father's vengeful rage. Incestuous desire is intrinsically agonizing; no conventional interdiction makes it so. It is the young man's desire that itself creates, out of its own inclinations, a horrible, anguish-generating monster.

See Jean-Joseph Goux, *Oedipus, Philosopher*, trans. Catherine Porter (Stanford: Stanford University Press, 1993), 36.

21. "It is Jewish, and not Greek," writes Harold Bloom, "to vacillate so dizzily between the need to be everything in oneself and the anxiety of being nothing in oneself. That vertigo is the condition that makes necessary what Freud called defense or repression, the flight from prohibited representations of desire." Bloom will see in Freud's fundamental dualism

> the Hebraic mode of dualism, which is not a split between mind or soul and body, or between the self and nature, but a subtler dichotomy between inwardness and outwardness. This is a prophetic dualism, the stance of Elijah and of the line of his successors from Amos to Malachi. In standing against the unjust world, Elijah and his disciples proclaim that justice must be established *against the world*, in a deep inwardness of morality that wars against all outwardness whatsoever. But what is this, in the Freudian register, except the moral basis for Freud's only transcendence, which is reality testing, or learning to live with the reality principle?

Bloom will go so far as to see a Gnostic or Kabalistic paradigm in Freud's catastrophe-theories. What is the origin of Freud's final dualism (Eros and Thanatos), Bloom convincingly asks, if it is not catastrophe? See Harold Bloom's "Introduction" and his essay "Freud's Concepts of Defense and of the Poetic Will" in *Sigmund Freud*, ed. Harold Bloom (New York: Chelsea House, 1985), 4, 157.

22. Samuel Weber, *The Legend of Freud* (Stanford: Stanford University Press, 2000), 146–47. See also Harold Bloom who takes this "nonperson" to another level: "In Freud, the fissure in us . . . insures that each of us is

her or his own worst enemy, exposed endlessly to the remorseless attacks of the superego, whose relation to the hapless ego is shockingly like the Gnostic vision of the relation of Yahweh to human beings." Harold Bloom, "Wrestling Sigmund," *The Breaking of the Vessels* (Chicago: The University of Chicago Press, 1982), 65.

23. For a brilliant analysis of "incorporation" (and its relation to introjection) see Jacques Derrida's discussion of the crypt in Nicolas Abraham and Maria Torok's *Le Verbier de l'homme aux loups*. Jacques Derrida, "Fors," in Nicolas Abraham and Maria Torok, *Le Verbier de l'homme aux loups* (Paris: Flammarion, 1976), 9–73. Along the lines of Derrida's reading, I would propose that we think of the emergence of the superego as the cryptic "non-lieu" that brings forth (*donne lieu*) the first judicial process. There is certainly a connection to be made between the juridical notion of a "non-lieu"—in which a trial is declared null and void and considered never to have taken place (in Freud's language one might say that the trial is "made unhappened")—and primary disavowal.

24. In "Notes upon a Case of Obsessional Neurosis," Freud gives us the case history of the Ratman, a case, which when "judged by its duration, the injuriousness of its effects, and the patient's own view of it" deserves to be classed as "moderately severe" (SE 10: 155). In addition to an obsession with his father's death, I would also point out that the Ratman creates an intricate web of obsessions around the repayment of a debt.

3. Flaubert: Testament to Disaster

1. Victor Brombert, *The Novels of Flaubert* (Princeton: Princeton University Press, 1966), 3.

2. When Flaubert learns from Louise Colet that she is not pregnant, he is jubilant:

> Je commence par te dévorer de baisers dans la joie qui me transporte. Ta lettre de ce matin m'a enlevé de dessus le cœur un terrible poids.... Il faudrait tout un livre pour développer d'une manière compréhensible mon sentiment à cet égard. L'idée de donner le jour à quelqu'un *me fait horreur*. Je me maudirais si j'étais père. –Un fils de moi, oh non, non, non! que toute ma chair périsse, et que je ne transmette à personne l'embêtement et les ignominies de l'existence. (CB 2: 205)

> I begin by devouring you with kisses, I am so overcome with joy. Your letter of this morning lifted a terrible weight from my heart.... It would take an entire

book to describe my feelings in this regard in a way that would be comprehensible. The idea of bringing someone into the world *fills me with horror.* I would curse myself were I a father. –A son of mine, oh no, no, no! may my flesh perish, and may I never transmit to another the boredom and the ignominies of existence.

3. Flaubert insists that he does not have the *right* to speak:

[J]'éprouve une répulsion invincible à mettre sur le papier quelque chose de mon cœur. Je trouve même qu'un romancier *n'a pas le droit d'exprimer son opinion* sur quoi que ce soit. Est-ce que Dieu l'a jamais dite, son opinion? (GS 107)

Un romancier, selon moi, *n'a pas le droit* de dire son avis sur les choses de ce monde. (CB 3: 517)

Quant à laisser voir mon opinion personnelle sur les gens que je mets en scène, non, non! mille fois non! Je ne m'en reconnais *pas le droit.* (GS 521)

[I] feel an invincible repulsion to putting anything of my heart on paper. I even think that a novelist *does not have the right to express his opinion* on anything whatsoever. Has God ever expressed his opinion?

A novelist, according to me, *does not have the right* to give his opinion on the things of this world.

As for revealing my personal opinion about the people I put on stage, no, no! a thousand times no! I *do not* recognize my *right* to do so.

An irreducible prohibition prevents Flaubert from speaking. Flaubert will call this irreducibility "justice"—

Est-ce qu'il n'est pas temps de faire entrer la Justice dans l'Art? L'impartialité de la Peinture atteindrait alors à la Majesté de la Loi, —et à la précision de la Science? (CB 3: 786)

[S]i nous sommes tellement bas moralement et politiquement, c'est qu'au lieu de suivre la grande route de M. de Voltaire, c'est-à-dire celle de la Justice et du Droit, on a pris les sentiers de Rousseau, qui, par le Sentiment, nous ont ramenés au Catholicisme. (CB 3: 720)

Is it not time for Justice to enter Art? The impartiality of painting would then approach the Majesty of the Law—and the precision of Science?

[I]f we are so low morally and politically, it is because instead of following the high road of M. de Voltaire, that is, the way of Justice and Right, we have taken the paths of Rousseau, which, through Sentiment, have returned us to Catholicism.

Where feeling—"le sentiment"—is everything and right—"le droit"—nothing, the very possibility of Art—"la grande route de M. de Voltaire"—has been lost. Justice and right are impartial where the heart is changeable, unpredictable and above all self-interested: "c'est une triste chose que ... d'analyser le cœur humain pour y trouver [l']égoïsme" (it is a sad thing indeed ... to analyze the human heart and find only egoism) (CB 1: 24). Indeed there is something downright obscene (Flaubert's repulsion is invincible) about the display of heart: "Laissez donc votre cœur et votre famille de côté et ne les détaillez pas au public!" (Leave aside your heart and your family and do not display them to the public!) he tells Louise Colet (CB 2: 554–55).

4. Although the four column article by Sainte-Beuve that appeared in *Le Moniteur universel* on May 4, 1857 was indeed and on the whole favorable to Flaubert, it nonetheless expressed some reserve: "Car, en bien des endroits et sous des formes diverses, je crois reconnaître des signes littéraires nouveaux: science, esprit d'observation, maturité, force, un peu de dureté. Ce sont des caractères que semblent affecter les chefs de file des générations nouvelles" (Indeed, in many places and in different forms, I begin to see new literary signs: science, a spirit of observation, maturity, force, a touch of harshness. These characteristics seem to affect the leaders of the new generations). Is there affectation in these new literary "signs"? Do these characteristics simply distinguish or mark the leaders of the new generation of writers or are they assumed, favored, but perhaps also somewhat—"un peu"—affected?

5. There is a constant sense of grievance in Flaubert's letters that one is never free to write what one wants. "Il est fort probable que je vais me rabattre sur *Les Deux Cloportes*. C'est une vieille idée que j'ai depuis des années et dont il faut peut-être que je me débarasse? J'aimerais mieux écrire un livre de passion. Mais on ne choisit pas ses sujets! on les subit" (It is very likely that I will fall back on *The Two Wood Lice*. It is an old idea I have had for years and should perhaps get rid of? I would prefer to write a book of passion. However, one does not choose one's subjects! one suffers them) (CB 3: 319–20); "Je ne fais rien de ce que je veux! Car on ne choisit pas ses sujets. Ils s'imposent" (Nothing I do is what I want! For one does not choose one's subjects. They impose themselves) (GS 209); "Nous ne sommes pas libres. Chacun suit sa voie, en dépit de sa propre volonté" (We are not free. Each follows his path in spite of his will) (GS 530).

6. In his discussion of German Romanticism in "L'Athenaeum," Maurice Blanchot speaks of the "non-romantic essence of romanticism" in

other terms. Maurice Blanchot, "L'Athenaeum," *L'entretien infini* (Paris: Gallimard, 1969), 524. I can do no more than suggest here that by remaining faithful to a legacy that is fatally contradictory in its injunctions, Flaubert's "style" might in fact be called an "allegory of Romanticism." For more on the contradictory essence of legacies in general, see in particular Derrida's discussion of Marx in "The Decontruction of Actuality": "To inherit is not essentially *to receive* something, a *given* that one could then *have*. It is an active affirmation; it responds to an injunction, but it also presupposes an initiative, the signature or countersignature of a critical selection. To inherit is to select, to sort, to highlight, to reactivate. I also think, although I cannot argue it here, that every assignation of legacy harbors a contradiction and a secret. . . . Whoever inherits chooses one spirit rather than another. One makes selections, one filters, one sifts through the ghosts or through the injunctions of each spirit. There is legacy only where assignations are multiple and contradictory, secret enough to defy interpretation, to carry the unlimited risk of active interpretation. . . . A legacy must retain an undecidable reserve." Jacques Derrida, "The Decontruction of Actuality," *Negotiations: Interventions and Interviews*, 1971–2001, ed. Elizabeth Rottenberg (Stanford: Stanford University Press, 2001), 110–11.

7. Paul de Man, "The Contemporary Criticism of Romanticism," *Romanticism and Contemporary Criticism*, eds. E. S. Burt, Kevin Newmark, and Andrzej Warminski (Baltimore and London: The Johns Hopkins University Press, 1993), 19.

8. Albert Thibaudet's article, "Le style de Flaubert," appeared in *La Nouvelle Revue Française* on December 1, 1919. Proust responds to this article with "À propos du 'style' de Flaubert" on January 1, 1920. Thibaudet will then respond to Proust's response in a "Lettre à Marcel Proust sur le style de Flaubert" in the same journal on March 1, 1920.

9. Albert Thibaudet, "Le style de Flaubert," *Sur Baudelaire, Flaubert et Morand*, ed. Antoine Compagnon (Paris: Éditions Complexe, 1987), 156.

10. Marcel Proust, "À propos du 'style' de Flaubert," *Écrits sur l'art*, ed. Jérôme Picon (Paris: Flammarion, 1999), 314. Henceforth all references will be abbreviated Pr and followed by a page number.

11. Albert Thibaudet, "Lettre à Marcel Proust sur le style de Flaubert," *Sur Baudelaire, Flaubert et Morand*, ed. Antoine Compagnon (Paris: Éditions Complexe, 1987), 176–77. Henceforth all references will be abbreviated Th and followed by a page number.

12. Proust's grammar does what it describes by showing what it is to move grammatically: from the lamp that ones moves to moving oneself both to and from a new house—moving the lamp has both a metonymic and a grammatical relation to moving in (proximity and apposition) but returning to the old house (in addition to apposition) requires that we literally return grammatically to its antecedent in the second metaphor. Grammar moves us forward and grammar moves us back: Proust's metaphor, in other words, remains wholly in the service of grammar.

13. The novelist and critic Barbey d'Aurevilly (Flaubert's fellow Norman)—who would later become one of Flaubert's most vicious critics—writes what is perhaps one of the most penetrating reviews of *Madame Bovary* where he notes, in order precisely to caution against it, Flaubert's impassibility:

> C'est un livre... sans tendresse.... M. Flaubert, lui, n'a point d'émotions; il n'a pas de jugement, du moins appréciable. C'est un narrateur incessant et infatigable, c'est un analyste qui ne se trouble jamais, c'est un *descripteur* jusqu'à la plus minutieuse subtilité. Mais il est sourd et muet d'impression à tout ce qu'il raconte. Il est indifférent à ce qu'il écrit avec le scrupule de l'amour. Si l'on forgeait à Birmingham ou à Manchester des machines à raconter ou à analyser en bon acier anglais qui fonctionneraient toutes seules par des procédés inconnus de dynamique, elles fonctionneraient absolument comme M. Flaubert. On sentirait dans ces machines autant de vie, d'âme, d'entrailles humaines que dans l'homme de marbre qui a écrit *Madame Bovary* avec une plume de pierre, comme le couteau des sauvages.
>
> Il répugne à la nature de l'homme d'avoir un sujet dans les mains sans se passionner pour ou contre. Mais M. Flaubert échappe à cette coutume qui semble une loi de l'esprit humain.
>
> Pour notre compte, nous ne connaissons pas de composition littéraire d'un talent plus vrai et qui soit en même temps plus dénuée d'enthousiasme, plus vide de cœur.
>
> It is a book... without tenderness.... M. Flaubert is a man without emotion; he does not judge, at least in any appreciable way. He is a relentless, tireless narrator, an analyst who never gets flustered, a *descriptor* down to the most painstaking detail. However, he is deaf and mute of impression to all that he recounts. He is indifferent to what he writes with the scrupulousness of a lover. Were one to forge narrating-analyzing machines in Birmingham or Manchester out of good English steel, machines that could function on their own by means of an unknown mechanism, they would function exactly in the

same way as M. Flaubert. One would feel in these machines just as much life, soul, human depth as in the man of marble who wrote *Madame Bovary* with a pen of stone, like the knife of savages.

It is repellant to human nature to have a subject without feeling passionately either for or against it. However, M. Flaubert escapes a custom that seems to be a law of the human spirit.

Personally, I know of no literary composition whose talent is truer and at the same time more devoid of enthusiasm, more empty of heart.

Barbey d'Aurevilly, *Le dix-neuvième siècle*, ed. Jacques Petit, 2 vols. (Paris: Mercure de France, 1964), 1, 205–07.

14. Gustave Flaubert, *L'Éducation sentimentale*, ed. Claudine Gothot-Mersch (Paris: Flammarion, 1985), 450.

[A]nd Frédéric, open-mouthed, recognized Sénécal.

> He traveled.
> He experienced the melancholy of steamboats, the cold dawns beneath his tent, the tedium of landscapes and ruins, the bitterness of interrupted sympathies.
> He returned.
> He frequented society...
> Towards the end of 1867...

15. In his oscillation between the blank at the end of Chapter 5 and "cet extraordinaire changement de vitesse, sans préparation" (the extraordinary change of gears, without preparation) (Pr 324) at the beginning of Chapter 6, Proust is not so much confusing ellipsis and acceleration—as Genette seems to suggest in his discussion of this passage—but describing the shock of surprise at their joint effect. See Gérard Genette, "Discours du récit," *Figures III* (Paris: Éditions du Seuil, 1972), 132–33.

16. Immanuel Kant, "Renewed Question: 'Is the Human Race Constantly Progressing Toward the Better?'" *The Conflict of the Faculties*, trans. Mary J. Gregor (Lincoln: University of Nebraska Press), 149.

17. Eugenio Donato makes a similar observation in slightly different terms: "[S]i par exemple *Madame Bovary* et *Salammbô* se terminent par une série de morts et si *La Tentation de Saint Antoine* et *Un cœur simple* finissent par des épiphanies fantasmatiques, ce n'est que dans *Bouvard et Pécuchet* que Flaubert renonce à "conclure".... D'où le caractère absolument unique de cette œuvre même dans le contexte du corpus des œuvres de Flaubert" (if, for example, *Madame Bovary* and *Salammbô* end

with a series of deaths, and if *The Temptation of Saint Anthony* and *A Simple Heart* finish with phantasmatic epiphanies, it is only in *Bouvard and Pécuchet* that Flaubert refuses to "conclude".... Whence the absolutely unique character of this work even within the context of Flaubert's corpus). See Eugenio Donato, "Qui Signe Flaubert?," *MLN* 98 (1983), note 590.

    18. Roland Barthes, "La crise de la vérité," *Œuvres complètes III* (Paris: Éditions du Seuil, 1995), 434.

    19. In his journal entry dated April 14, 1887, Flaubert's longtime friend Edmond de Goncourt notes the discovery of Maurice's ten page article: "On parcourt chez Daudet, avant dîner, cet article du *Journal des Journaux,* signé B. Maurice, d'où Flaubert a tiré l'idée de son roman de *Bouvard et Pécuchet. Il ne peut y avoir de doute . . . les deux bonshommes qui recopient . . . la vie plate comme le canal Saint-Martin . . . et tout enfin. C'est bien curieux que Flaubert n'ait pas été arrêté par la prévision qu'un jour ou l'autre, cette espèce de plagiat serait découvert" (Before dinner at Daudet's, we glance through the article in the *Journal des Journaux* signed B. Maurice where Flaubert got the idea for his novel *Bouvard and Pécuchet.* There can be no doubt about it . . . the two copyists . . . life as *flat as the Saint-Martin canal . . .* everything, in the end. It is very curious that Flaubert should not have been inhibited by the knowledge that one day or another this kind of plagiarism would be discovered). See Edmond and Jules de Goncourt, *Journal,* 3 vols. (Paris: Robert Laffont, 1989), 3, 31. I would suggest that this friendly fire, displaced as it is onto the question of plagiarism, allowed de Goncourt to express his great ambivalence about the novel, indirectly.

    20. Claudine Gothot-Mersch, "Introduction," *Bouvard et Pécuchet* (Paris: Gallimard, 1979), 13.

    21. Jean-Paul Sartre, *L'Idiot de la famille,* 3 vols. (Paris: Gallimard, 1971–1972), 3, 656. For a truly original reading of Sartre's reading of Flaubert, see Neil Hertz, "Flaubert's Conversion," *Gustave Flaubert,* ed. Harold Bloom (New York and Philadelphia: Chelsea House Publishers, 1989), 63–74.

    22. Henry Céard, "Portraits littéraires: Gustave Flaubert," cited in René Dumesnil's "Introduction" to *Bouvard et Pécuchet* (Paris: Société les Belles Lettres, 1945), CLXIX.

    23. "[I]l n'y a pas, dans *Bouvard et Pécuchet* . . . de plan allocutoire: personne ne s'adresse à personne, et on ne sait jamais d'où part et où va le message. Eux-mêmes, les deux personnages . . . ne s'adressent jamais

la parole. Et ce couple, ce bloc amoureux qu'ils forment... est lointain, glacé, et ne s'adresse pas au lecteur. Le livre ne s'adresse pas à nous, et c'est précisément ce qui peut gêner.... Pour moi, c'est cette perte de l'allocutoire, de l'adresse—intercommunication qui existe dans tout livre écrit, même à la troisième personne—qui est fascinante, parce qu'elle est, en germe, le discours du psychotique" (there is no allocutionary plan in *Bouvard and Pécuchet*: no one is addressing anyone, and we never know where the message is coming from or where it goes. Even the two characters... do not address each other. Moreover, the couple, the amorous block they form... is remote, chilly, and does not address the reader. The book does not address us, and this is precisely what is disturbing about it.... Personally, the loss of the allocutionary, of address—the intercommunication that exists in any written book, even in the third person—is what I find so fascinating, because it is the beginning of a psychotic discourse). See Roland Barthes, "La crise de la vérité," *Œuvres complètes III* (Paris: Éditions du Seuil, 1995), 435.

24. J. Barbey d'Aurevilly, *Le Roman contemporain* (Paris: Lemerre, 1902), 131–33.

25. In Flaubert's famous 1850 letter to Louis Bouilhet in which he holds forth against the positivism of Auguste Comte, he writes the following: "*L'ineptie consiste à vouloir conclure....* c'est de ne pas comprendre le crépuscule, c'est ne vouloir que midi ou minuit.... Oui, la bêtise consiste à vouloir conclure" (Ineptitude consists in wanting to conclude.... It is a misunderstanding of twilight, a desire only for noon or midnight.... Yes, stupidity consists in wanting to conclude) (CB 1: 679).

26. Barbey d'Aurevilly's own relation to the "bourgeois" is highly ambivalent, to say the least. Not only does he presuppose ("assume") Flaubert's hatred of the bourgeois to inveigh against *Bouvard et Pécuchet*, but he also appropriates ("assumes") Flaubert's hatred of the bourgeois to rail against other writers, namely Goethe and Diderot. Barbey d'Aurevilly's constant harping about the "bourgeois" ends up provoking Zola: "M. Barbey d'Aurevilly, à la longue, devient terriblement agaçant à traiter les gens de bourgeois. Nous sommes tous des bourgeois. Goethe, bourgeois! Diderot, bourgeois! Eh! monsieur, bourgeois vous-même, puisque bourgeois est une injure!.... Oui, bourgeois, et, qui plus est, bourgeois de province!" (In the end M. Barbey d'Aurevilly becomes terribly irritating by calling everyone a "bourgeois." We are all bourgeois. Goethe, borgeois! Diderot, bourgeois! Ah! sir, bourgeois yourself, since bourgeois is an insult!.... Yes, bourgeois, and, what is more, a bourgeois

from the provinces!). See Émile Zola, *Face aux romantiques*, ed. Henri Mittérand (Paris: Éditions Complexe, 1989), 66.

27. "La fin de *Candide*: 'Cultivons notre jardin' est la plus grande leçon de morale qui existe" (The end of *Candide*: "Let us cultivate our garden" is the greatest moral lesson that exists). *Correspondance Gustave Flaubert–les Goncourt*, ed. Pierre-Jean Dufief (Paris: Flammarion, 1998), 248.

28. Flaubert had originally projected a second volume for *Bouvard et Pécuchet* that would have been composed of his own reading notes for *Bouvard et Pécuchet*: "The Copy" of the two clerks, which was to have contained a collage of quotations from books previously read and idiotic excerpts from critical works of all kinds. Much has been written on what this second volume might have looked like. For the most comprehensive discussion of the documents related to this volume, see Claude Mouchard and Jacques Neefs, "Vers le second volume: *Bouvard et Pécuchet*," *Flaubert à l'œuvre* (Paris: Flammarion, 1980), 171–217.

29. Jean-Pierre Moussaron, "Une étrange greffe," *Limites des Beaux-Arts* (Paris: Galilée, 1999). See in particular Part 2: "En fait, occurrence la plus fréquente du discours de savoir dans l'œuvre, cette diction au présent intemporel à valeur impersonnelle d'objectivité scientifique se dégage de toute assignation univoque; tandis que l'absence de guillemets détruit la démarcation nette entre discours d'accueil et discours accuelli" (Indeed, as the most frequent occurrence of encyclopedic discourse in the book, the speech that takes place in the intemporal present and whose impersonal value of is that of scientific objectivity frees itself of any univocal assignation while the absence of quotation marks eliminates the clear demarcation between host language and language cited) (116–17).

30. See Jacques Neefs, "Le volume des livres," *L'Arc* 79, special issue on Gustave Flaubert, 78.

31. Gustave Flaubert, *Bouvard and Pécuchet*, trans. A. J. Krailsheimer (New York: Penguin Books, 1976), 83.

32. Flaubert literally referred to Chapter 1 as a "Prologue," a reference that has occasioned some confusion and much critical debate. "J'aurai le temps, d'ici là, de mettre bien en train mon premier chapitre (celui de l'agriculture), lequel commence à se dessiner nettement dans mon imaginative. –Mon Prologue sera fait demain. Il me manque, pour l'avoir fini, de m'être promené la nuit avec une chandelle dans le potager, excursion que je vais accomplir ce soir" (Between now and then I'll have enough time to get my first chapter under way (the chapter on agriculture), which is beginning to take shape in my imagination. –My

Prologue will be done tomorrow. To finish it, I still need to take a walk by candlelight through the vegetable garden, an excursion I will undertake this evening) (CB 4: 877).

33. "Turgeniev is lecturing me about getting back to work on my big book about the two Wood Lice. He is quite taken with it. But the difficulties of such a book overwhelm me. And yet I do not want to die without having done it. For when all is said and done, it is my *testament*." (GS 524, my emphasis)

34. In a most surprising article, Eugenio Donato discusses the way in which Flaubert subscribes to a view of history that assumes a temporality similar to that predicated by the new physics. "The revolution introduced by thermodynamics is a revolution at the very heart of history. The second principle, so striking to the Romantic imagination, states that energy goes from a differentiated to an undifferentiated state. The consequences are enormous; henceforth, systems will move inexorably in a given direction." See Eugenio Donato, "The Museum's Furnace: Notes Toward a Contextual Reading of *Bouvard and Pécuchet*," *The Script of Decadence* (Oxford: Oxford University Press, 1993), 73.

35. Jacques Neefs, "De Flaubert à Pérec," *Théorie Littérature Enseignement* 5 (1987): 39.

36. Marcel Proust, "Sainte-Beuve et Balzac," *Contre Sainte-Beuve* (Paris: Gallimard, 1954), 201.

37. "Quelle chienne de chose que la prose! Ça n'est jamais fini" (prose is a dog-gone thing! It is never finished!) (CB 2: 135); "Voilà ce que la prose a de diabolique, c'est qu'elle n'est jamais finie" (This is what is diabolical about prose, it is never finished) (CB 2: 364).

38. "L'auteur, dans son œuvre, doit être comme Dieu dans l'univers, présent partout, et visible nulle part. L'art étant une seconde nature, le créateur de cette nature-là doit agir par des procédés analogues: que l'on sente dans tous les atomes, à tous les aspects, une impassibilité cachée et infinie. L'effet, pour le spectateur, doit être une espèce d'ébahissement. Comment tout cela s'est-il fait! doit-on dire! et qu'on se sente écrasé sans savoir pourquoi" (The author in his work must be like God in the universe, present everywhere and visible nowhere. Art being a second nature, the creator of that nature must make use of similar procedures: let there be sensed in every atom, in every aspect, a hidden and infinite impassivity. The effect for the spectator must be a kind of shock. How was it all done! one must say! And one should feel crushed without knowing why) (CB 2: 204).

39. Maurice Blanchot, "Le problème de Wittgenstein," *L'entretien infini* (Paris: Gallimard, 1969), 490.

Postscript: Last Words

1. Paul de Man, "Excuses (Confessions)," *Allegories of Reading* (New Haven: Yale University Press, 1979), 294. All further references to this text will be abbreviated AR followed by page number.

2. Paul de Man, "Kant and Schiller," *Aesthetic Ideology* (Minneapolis: University of Minnesota Press, 1996), 132–33. All further references to this text will be abbreviated AI followed by page number.

3. Jacques Derrida, "Typewriter Ribbon: Limited Ink (2) ('within such limits')," *Material Events*, eds. Tom Cohen, Barbara Cohen, J. Hillis Miller, and Andrzej Warminski, trans. Peggy Kamuf (Minneapolis: University of Minnesota Press, 2001), 319. All further references to this text will be abbreviated TR followed by page number.

4. Jacques Derrida, "Le ruban de machine à écrire," *Papier Machine* (Paris: Galilée, 2001), 91.

5. Barbey d'Aurevilly, *Le dix-neuvième siècle*, ed. Jacques Petit, 2 vols. (Paris: Mercure de France, 1964), 1, 205–07. See also note 13 of Chapter 3.

6. Maurice Blanchot, *L'instant de ma mort* (Cognac: Fata Morgana, 1994), 20.

Works Cited

Allison, Henry. *The Kant–Eberhard Controversy.* Baltimore: Johns Hopkins University Press, 1973.

———. *Kant's Theory of Freedom.* Cambridge: Cambridge University Press, 1990.

———. *Idealism and Freedom.* Cambridge: Cambridge University Press, 1996.

Austin, John Langshaw. *How to Do Things with Words.* Cambridge: Harvard University Press, 1962.

Barbey d'Aurevilly, Jules. *Le Roman contemporain.* Paris: Lemerre, 1902.

———. *Le dix-neuvième siècle.* Ed. Jacques Petit. 2 vols. Paris: Mercure de France, 1964.

Barthes, Roland. *Œuvres complètes III.* Paris: Éditions du Seuil, 1995.

Bass, Alan. *Difference and Disavowal: The Trauma of Eros.* Stanford: Stanford University Press, 2000.

Bennington, Geoffrey. *Frontières kantiennes.* Paris: Galilée, 2000.

Blanchot, Maurice. *L'entretien infini.* Paris: Gallimard, 1969.

———. *L'instant de ma mort.* Cognac: Fata Morgana, 1994.

Bloom, Harold. *The Breaking of the Vessels.* Chicago: The University of Chicago Press, 1982.

———. "Freud's Concepts of Defense and the Poetic Will." In *Sigmund Freud,* ed. Harold Bloom, 143–62. New York: Chelsea House, 1985.

Brombert, Victor. *The Novels of Flaubert.* Princeton: Princeton University Press, 1966.

de Man, Paul. "Semiology and Rhetoric." In *Allegories of Reading: Figural Language in Rousseau, Nietzsche, Rilke, and Proust*, 3–19. New Haven: Yale University Press, 1979.

——. "Excuses (Confessions)." In *Allegories of Reading: Figural Language in Rousseau, Nietzsche, Rilke, and Proust*, 278–301. New Haven: Yale University Press, 1979.

——. "Aesthetic Formalization: Kleist's *Über das Marionettentheater.*" In *Rhetoric of Romanticism*, 263–90. New York: Columbia University Press, 1984.

——. "The Resistance to Theory." In *The Resistance to Theory*, 3–20. Minneapolis: University of Minnesota Press, 1986.

——. "The Contemporary Criticism of Romanticism." In *Romanticism and Contemporary Criticism*, eds. E. S. Burt, Kevin Newmark, and Andrzej Warminski, 3–24. Baltimore and London: The Johns Hopkins University Press, 1993.

——. "Phenomenality and Materiality in Kant." In *Aesthetic Ideology*, ed. Andrzej Warminski, 70–90. Minneapolis: University of Minnesota Press, 1996.

——. "Kant's Materialism." In *Aesthetic Ideology*, ed. Andrzej Warminski, 119–28. Minneapolis: University of Minnesota Press, 1996.

——. "Kant and Schiller." In *Aesthetic Ideology*, ed. Andrzej Warminski, 129–62. Minneapolis: University of Minnesota Press, 1996.

Derrida, Jacques. "Fors." In Nicolas Abraham and Maria Torok, *Le Verbier de l'homme aux loups*, 9–73. Paris: Flammarion, 1976.

——. "Deconstruction in America: An Interview with Jacques Derrida." *Critical Exchange* 17 (Winter 1985): 1–33.

——. "The Deconstruction of Actuality." In *Negotiations: Interventions and Interviews 1971–2001*, ed. Elizabeth Rottenberg, 85–116. Stanford: Stanford University Press, 2001.

——. "On the 'Priceless,' or the 'Going Rate' of the Transaction." In *Negotiations: Interventions and Interviews 1971–2001*, ed. Elizabeth Rottenberg, 315–28. Stanford: Stanford University Press, 2001.

——. "Le ruban de machine à écrire." In *Papier Machine*, 33–147. Paris: Galilée, 2001.

——. "Typewriter Ribbon: Limited Ink (2) ('within such limits')." In *Material Events*, eds. Tom Cohen, Barbara Cohen, J. Hillis Miller and Andrzej Warminski, trans. Peggy Kamuf, 277–360. Minneapolis: University of Minnesota Press, 2001.

Donato, Eugenio. *The Script of Decadence.* Oxford: Oxford University Press, 1993.

Fenves, Peter. *A Peculiar Fate: Metaphysics and World-History in Kant.* Ithaca: Cornell University Press, 1991.

Ferenczi, Sandor. *First Contributions to Psychoanalysis.* New York: Bruner-Mazel, 1980.

Flaubert, Gustave. *Bouvard et Pécuchet.* Ed. Claudine Gothot-Mersch. Paris: Gallimard, 1979.

———. *Bouvard and Pécuchet.* Trans. T. W. Earp and G. W. Stonier. New York: New Directions, 1954.

———. *Bouvard and Pécuchet.* Trans. A. J. Krailsheimer. New York: Penguin Books, 1976.

———. *L'Éducation sentimentale.* Ed. Claudine Gothot-Mersch. Paris: Flammarion, 1985.

———. *Correspondance.* Eds. René Dumesnil, Jean Pommier, and Claude Digeon. 9 vols. Paris: Conard, 1926–1933.

———. *Correspondance.* Eds. René Dumesnil, Jean Pommier, and Claude Digeon. 4 vols. supplement. Paris: Conard, 1954.

———. *Correspondance.* Ed. Jean Bruneau. 4 vols. Paris: Gallimard, 1973–1998.

———. *Correspondance Gustave Flaubert–George Sand.* Ed. Alphonse Jacobs. Paris: Flammarion, 1981.

———. *Correspondance Gustave Flaubert–Ivan Tourguéniev.* Ed. Alexandre Zviguilsky. Paris: Flammarion, 1989.

———. *Correspondance Gustave Flaubert–Guy de Maupassant.* Ed. Yvan Leclerc. Paris: Flammarion, 1993.

———. *Correspondance Gustave Flaubert–les Goncourt.* Ed. Pierre-Jean Dufief. Paris: Flammarion, 1998.

Freud, Sigmund. *The Standard Edition of the Complete Psychological Works of Sigmund Freud.* Trans. James Strachey in collaboration with Anna Freud, assisted by Alix Strachey and Alan Tyson. 24 vols. London: The Hogarth Press, 1953–1974.

———. *Project for a Scientific Psychology.* SE 1. 295–397.

———. "The Neuro-Psychoses of Defense." SE 3. 43–68.

———. *The Interpretation of Dreams.* SE 4–5. 1–625.

———. "Notes upon a Case of Obsessional Neurosis." SE 10. 155–318.

———. "Formulations on the Two Principles of Mental Functioning." SE 12. 218–26.

———. "Instincts and their Vicissitudes." SE 14. 117–40.

———. "A Difficulty in the Path of Psychoanalysis." SE 17. 136–44.

———. *Beyond the Pleasure Principle.* SE 18. 7–64.

———. "Group Psychology and the Analysis of the Ego." SE 18. 69–143.

———. *The Ego and the Id.* SE 19. 12–66.

———. "Neurosis and Psychosis." SE 19. 149–53.

———. "The Loss of Reality in Neurosis and Psychosis." SE 19. 183–87.

———. "Inhibitions, Symptoms and Anxiety." SE 20. 87–172.

———. *The Future of an Illusion.* SE 21. 3–58.

———. *Civilization and Its Discontents.* SE 21. 64–145.

———. "Fetishism." SE 21. 152–57.

———. *An Outline of Psychoanalysis.* SE 23. 144–206.

———. "Splitting of the Ego in the Process of Defense." SE 23. 271–76.

Genette, Gérard. *Figures III.* Paris: Éditions du Seuil, 1972.

Goux, Jean-Joseph. *Oedipus, Philosopher.* Trans. Catherine Porter. Stanford: Stanford University Press, 1993.

Hamacher, Werner. *Pleroma—zu Genesis and Struktur einer dialektischen Hermeneutik bei Hegel.* Frankfurt am Main: Ullstein, 1978.

———. "Afformative, Strike." In *Walter Benjamin's Philosophy: Destruction and Experience,* eds. Andrew Benjamin and Peter Osbourne, trans. Dana Hollander, 110–38. London and New York: Routledge, 1994.

———. *Premises.* Trans. Peter Fenves. Cambridge: Harvard University Press, 1996.

Hanson, Norwood Russell. "Copernicus's Role in Kant's Revolution." *Journal of the History of Ideas* 20 (1959): 274–81.

Hegel, G. W. F. *Werke.* Eds. Eva Moldenhauer and Karl Markus Michel. 20 vols. Frankfurt am Main: Suhrkamp, 1971.

Heidegger, Martin. *Der Satz vom Grund.* Pfullingen: Neske, 1957.

———. *Kant und das Problem der Metaphysik.* Frankfurt am Main: Klostermann, 1973.

———. *Schellings Abhandlung Über das Wesen der menschlichen Freiheit.* Tübingen: Niemeyer, 1995.

Hertz, Neil. "Flaubert's Conversion." In *Gustave Flaubert,* ed. Harold Bloom, 63–74. New York and Philadelphia: Chelsea House Publishers, 1989.

Kant, Immanuel. *Kants Gesammelte Schriften.* Ed. Königliche Preussische (later Deutsche) Akademie der Wissenschaften. 29 vols. Berlin and Leipzig: Walter de Gruyer, 1902.

———. *Critique of Practical Reason.* Trans. L. W. Beck. Indianapolis: Bobbs-Merrill, 1956.

———. *Religion within the Limits of Reason Alone.* Trans. Theodore M. Greene and Hoyt H. Hudson. New York: Harper and Row, 1960.

———. *Groundwork of the Metaphysic of Morals.* Trans. H. J. Paton. New York: Harper Torchbooks, 1964.

———. *Critique of Pure Reason.* Trans. Norman Kemp Smith. New York: St. Martin's Press, 1965.

———. "What Is Orientation in Thinking?" In *Political Writings,* ed. Hans Reiss, trans. H. B. Nisbet, 237–49. New York: Cambridge University Press, 1991.

———. *The Metaphysics of Morals.* Trans. Mary Gregor. Cambridge: Cambridge University Press, 1991.

———. *The Conflict of the Faculties.* Trans. Mary Gregor. Nebraska: University of Nebraska Press, 1992.

———. *Grounding for the Metaphysics, of Morals.* Trans. James M. Ellington. Indianapolis: Hackett, 1993.

———. *Lectures on Ethics.* Eds. Peter Heath and J. B. Schneewind. Trans. Peter Heath. Cambridge and New York: Cambridge University Press, 1997.

———. "On a Newly Arisen Superior Tone in Philosophy." In *Raising the Tone of Philosophy,* ed. and trans. Peter Fenves, 51–82. Baltimore: Johns Hopkins University Press, 1998.

Kaulbach, Friedrich. "Die Kopernikanische Denkfigur bei Kant." *Kant-Studien* 64 (1973): 30–48.

Lacan, Jacques. *Écrits.* Paris: Éditions du Seuil, 1966.

Laplanche, Jean. *La révolution copernicienne inachevée.* Paris: Aubier, 1992.

———. *Entre séduction et inspiration: l'homme.* Paris: Presses Universitaires de France, 1999.

Mouchard, Claude and Neefs, Jacques. "Vers le second volume: *Bouvard et Pécuchet.*" In *Flaubert à l'œuvre,* 171–217. Paris: Flammarion, 1980.

Moussaron, Jean-Pierre. *Limites des Beaux-Arts.* Paris: Galilée, 1999.

Prauss, Gerold. *Kant über Freiheit als Autonomie.* Frankfurt am Main: Klostermann, 1983.

Proust, Marcel. *Contre Sainte-Beuve.* Paris: Gallimard, 1954.

———. *Écrits sur l'art.* Ed. Jérôme Picon. Paris: Flammarion, 1999.

Rapoport, Judith L. *The Boy Who Couldn't Stop Washing.* New York: Penguin Books, 1990.

Rawls, John. *A Theory of Justice.* Cambridge: Harvard University Press, 1971.

Rose, Jacqueline. "Just, Lasting, Comprehensive." In *States of Fantasy,* 78–95. Oxford: Oxford University Press, 1996.

Sartre, Jean-Paul. *L'Idiot de la famille.* 3 vols. Paris: Gallimard, 1971–1972.

Schneewind, J. B. "Autonomy, Obligation, and Virtue: An Overview of Kant's Moral Philosophy." In *The Cambridge Companion to Kant,* ed. Paul Guyer, 309–41. Cambridge: Cambridge University Press, 1992.

Thibaudet, Albert. "Une querelle littéraire sur le style de Flaubert." In Marcel Proust, *Sur Baudelaire, Flaubert et Morand,* ed. Antoine Compagnon, 153–68. Paris: Éditions Complexe, 1987.

———. "Lettre à Marcel Proust sur le style de Flaubert." In Marcel Proust, *Sur Baudelaire, Flaubert et Morand,* ed. Antoine Compagnon, 171–97. Paris: Éditions Complexe, 1987.

Weber, Samuel. *Return to Freud.* Trans. Michael Levine. Cambridge: Cambridge University Press, 1991.

———. *The Legend of Freud.* Stanford: Stanford University Press, 2000.

Zola, Émile. *Face aux romantiques.* Ed. Henri Mittérand. Paris: Éditions Complexe, 1989.

Index

Crossing Aesthetics

Shoshana Felman, *The Scandal of the Speaking Body: Don Juan with J. L. Austin, or Seduction in Two Languages*

Peter Szondi, *Celan Studies*

Neil Hertz, *George Eliot's Pulse*

Maurice Blanchot, *The Book to Come*

Susannah Young-ah Gottlieb, *Regions of Sorrow: Anxiety and Messianism in Hannah Arendt and W. H. Auden*

Jaques Derrida, *Without Alibi, edited by Peggy Kamuf*

Cornelius Castoriadis, *On Plato's 'Statesman'*

Jacques Derrida, *Who's Afraid of Philosophy? Right to Philosophy 1*

Peter Szondi, *An Essay on the Tragic*

Peter Fenves, *Arresting Language: From Leibniz to Benjamin*

Jill Robbins, ed. *Is It Righteous to Be?: Interviews with Emmanuel Levinas*

Louis Marin, *Of Representation*

Daniel Payot, *The Architect and the Philosopher*

J. Hillis Miller, *Speech Acts in Literature*

Maurice Blanchot, *Faux pas*

Jean-Luc Nancy, *Being Singular Plural*

Maurice Blanchot/Jacques Derrida, *The Instant of My Death/Demeure: Fiction and Testimony*

Niklas Luhmann, *Art as a Social System*

Emmanual Levinas, *God, Death, and Time*

Ernst Bloch, *The Spirit of Utopia*

Giorgio Agamben, *Potentialities: Collected Essays in Philosophy*

Serge Leclaire, *A Child Is Being Killed: On Primary Narcissism and the Death Drive*

Sigmund Freud, *Writings on Art and Literature*

Cornelius Castoriadis, *World in Fragments: Writings on Politics, Society, Psychoanalysis, and the Imagination*

Thomas Keenan, *Fables of Responsibility: Aberrations and Predicaments in Ethics and Politics*

Emmanuel Levinas, *Proper Names*

Alexander García Düttmann, *At Odds with AIDS: Thinking and Talking About a Virus*

Maurice Blanchot, *Friendship*

Jean-Luc Nancy, *The Muses*

Massimo Cacciari, *Posthumous People: Vienna at the Turning Point*

David E. Wellbery, *The Specular Moment: Goethe's Early Lyric and the Beginnings of Romanticism*

Edmond Jabès, *The Little Book of Unsuspected Subversion*

Hans-Jost Frey, *Studies in Poetic Discourse: Mallarmé, Baudelaire, Rimbaud, Hölderlin*

Pierre Bourdieu, *The Rules of Art: Genesis and Structure of the Literary Field*

Nicolas Abraham, *Rhythms: On the Work, Translation, and Psychoanalysis*

Jacques Derrida, *On the Name*

David Wills, *Prosthesis*

Maurice Blanchot, *The Work of Fire*

Jacques Derrida, *Points . . . : Interviews, 1974–1994*